Introducing The Cotswolds

Other books by Charles and Alice Mary Hadfield

The Cotswolds
The Cotswolds: A New Study (editors)

by Charles Hadfield

British Canals
Introducing Inland Waterways

by Alice Mary Hadfield

The Chartist Land Company
King Arthur and the Round Table

Introducing
The Cotswolds

Charles Hadfield
Alice Mary Hadfield

David & Charles Newton Abbot London

North Pomfret (VT) Vancouver

ISBN 0 7153 7169 x
Library of Congress
Catalog Card Number 76-2149

Set in 11 on 13 pt Baskerville
by TRI-AM Photoset Limited,
Bridge Foot, Warrington
and printed in Great Britain
by Morrison & Gibb Limited, Edinburgh
for David & Charles (Publishers) Limited
Brunel House Newton Abbot Devon

Published in the United States of America
by David & Charles Inc
North Pomfret Vermont 05053 USA

Published in Canada
by Douglas David & Charles Limited
1875 Welch Street North Vancouver BC

CONTENTS

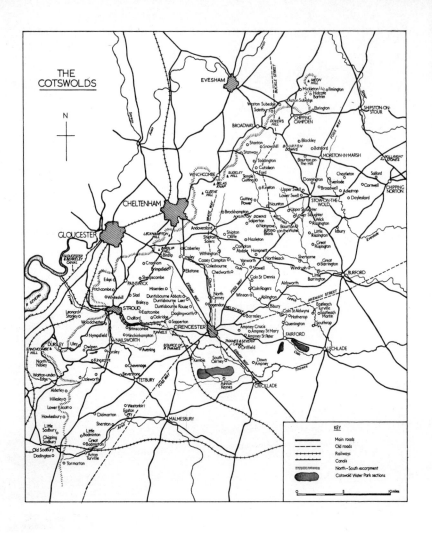

THE COTSWOLDS

N

EVESHAM

MEON HILL
Mickleton Hidcote Bartrim
Ilmington

Weston Subedge
Saintsby
Aston Subedge
Ebrington
SHIPSTON-ON-STOUR

CHIPPING CAMPDEN

BROADWAY

Blockley
Batsford
Snowshill
Stanton
Bourton-on-the-Hill
MORETON-IN-MARSH

Strawway
Taddington
Cutsdean
Ford

WINCHCOMBE
Temple Guiting
Kineton
Upper Swell
Lower Swell
Donnington
Charlton
Evenlode
Cornwell
ROLLRIGHT STONES

CHIPPING NORTON

Guiting Power
Naunton
Upper Slaughter
Lower Slaughter
Broadwell
Adlestrop
Daylesford

CHELTENHAM

Brockhampton
Salperton
Notgrove
Aston Blank
Bourton on the Water
Wick Rissington
Idbury

GLOUCESTER

Andoversford
Shipton Solers
Shipton Oliffe
Hazleton
Northleach
Little Rissington
Great Rissington

Coberley
Birdlip
Withington
Compton Abdale
Hampnett
Sherborne
Great Barrington

Cassey Compton
Colesbourne
Yanworth
Stowell
Windrush
BURFORD

Cranham
Elkstone
Chedworth
Coln St Dennis
Aldsworth
Barrington

Edge
Pitchcombe
Sheepscombe
Misarden
Coln Rogers
Winson
Ablington
Eastleach Turville
Eastleach Martin

PAINSWICK
Slad
Bisley
Duntisbourne Abbots
Duntisbourne Leer
Duntisbourne Rouse
Daglingworth
North Cerney
Barnsley
Bibury
Coln St Aldwyn
Hatherop
Southrop

STROUD
Chalford
Eastcombe
Oakridge
Bagendon
Quenington

Brimscombe
Sapperton
Ampney Crucis
Ampney St Mary
Ampney St Peter
FAIRFORD

NAILSWORTH
Minchinhampton
CIRENCESTER
Driffield

DURSLEY
Uley
Owlpen
Dursley
Chavenage
Kemble
South Cerney
Down Ampney
LECHLADE

North Nibley
Kingscote
Beverston
Cricklade
Ashton Keynes

Watton-under-Edge
Ozleworth
TETBURY

Alderley
Hillesley
Lower Kilcott
Hawkesbury
Westonbirt
Easton Grey

Little Sodbury
Didmarton
Sherston
MALMESBURY

Great Sodbury
Little Badminton
Great Badminton

Chipping Sodbury
Old Sodbury
Dodington
Acton Turville
Tormarton

KEY

—————— Main roads
– – – – – Old roads
+–+–+–+ Railways
+++++++ Canals
ıııııııı North–South escarpment
🌑 Cotswold Water Park sections

0   5   10 miles

Introduction

The Cotswolds are a formation of smooth hills, the highest just over 1,000ft, rising up from the heart of England. In the north they begin at Meon Hill, five miles south of Stratford-upon-Avon, and run for about forty miles south-west to the approaches to Bristol and Bath. One cannot accurately draw a circle and say 'inside that are the Cotswolds,' for no two people would agree on their boundaries. Our own limits for the purpose of this book are shown on the map on p. 6.

The landscape and architecture of the Cotswolds arise out of the particular kind of limestone of which they are formed, which is different from the limestone to the south, east and north. The Cotswold kind is oolitic, and is formed of shells of sea creatures and sand of the ancient curious age when England was at the bottom of the sea. It is not hard and rocky, but made up of particles which, under the turf, are easily moulded by frost, rain and wind into smooth, subtle lines, leaving few rugged or dramatic features. When dug up and exposed, it develops a resistant quality and a sensitivity to light as varying as its myriad-particle make-up.

The Cotswolds are shaped like a slice of cake lying on its side: the broad side, called the escarpment, rises up steeply on the north and west in a green wall from Meon Hill, past the great central mass of Cleeve, Leckhampton, Charlton Kings and Birdlip Hills above Cheltenham and Gloucester, to the re-entrants of the Stroud and Nailsworth valleys with Rodborough and Minchinhampton Commons high between them, and on to Stinchcombe Hill and the heights above Wotton-under-Edge. Then it slowly sinks and merges into other limestone country. Great beechwoods clothe the middle escarpment, their centre at Cranham.

East and south the land slopes gently down from the escarpment, forming the central wolds from Chedworth and

Sapperton across to Bourton-on-the-Water and Burford, then levelling out towards Moreton-in-Marsh, Fairford, Lechlade, Cirencester and the developing gravel-bearing areas on the south. Five Cotswold rivers, Evenlode, Windrush, Leach, Coln and Churn, run off south to join the Thames; three others, Frome, Nailsworth Avon and Bristol Avon, run west to join the Severn. Their valleys offer experiences very different from the uplands.

The Cotswolds mean also a style of architecture. The oolitic limestone makes a building material which is responsive and workable when first dug, but which hardens after exposure to stand for centuries. Stone roofing slates or tiles are used with it on almost all old, and many new, buildings. These used to be found in layers in their own quarries. They were lifted out and then left exposed all winter, after which they could be split along the cracks and then chipped into many different sizes, each of which bore an identifying name. The basic colour and delicate variations of this roofing material are an incomparable beauty. Tiling is done in graded sizes across the area, smallest at the roof-tree and biggest at the eaves, giving liveliness and delicacy to the work. Each slate used to be held with a particular small bone of a sheep, but now usually by a copper pin.

The limestone supports all lime-loving growth. These wolds are known for their beeches, thick on the escarpment or in Cirencester Park, or in mushroom-shaped clumps and long windbreaks over the country, mixed with chestnut, sycamore and larch. Hawthorn, wayfaring tree (viburnum), briar rose and dogwood are thick in the hedges, and blue geranium on verges and along the barley or wheat fields. Long lines of low stone walls chequer the high wolds where the turf, clean and thin, makes fine, healthy grazing for sheep.

On the whole we have kept in this book to the high land and to those places just off it which share its character, like Inglesham because of its wonderful little church, or South Cerney because we have called it home. The southern boundary is the most difficult to draw, yet somewhere between Didmarton and Bath the Cotswolds end; we have taken the M4 as the boundary.

Alice Mary, who has written the text of this book, was born, bred and educated in and around the Cotswolds: Charles came to them from Africa, Devonshire and London, first on holidays with his family, then as a resident.

Each chapter of *Introducing the Cotswolds* describes a tour by car round a part of the area, beginning and ending at a small place interesting in itself and provided with at least one good hotel in or near it. Tours can, however, be broken into, or out of, at any point, or the second part of one linked to the first part of the next. An outline map illustrates each chapter, but we strongly suggest that those who use this book for touring should buy the OS 1:50,000 sheets for the area. Those needed are listed at the end of each chapter, but seven, Nos 150, 151, 162, 163, 164, 172 and 173 cover the whole of the Cotswolds. With these and the chapter maps you will not get lost.

The main body of the Cotswolds is in Gloucestershire, but its edges touch other counties: Hereford and Worcester at Broadway, for instance, but also Warwickshire, Oxfordshire, Berkshire, Wiltshire and Avon. Most of it was designated an Area of Outstanding Natural Beauty in 1966. Its character will, we hope, come through the printed pages of this book and be shown in the illustrations.

Living all the year round at South Cerney, we often felt it a pity that so many people saw the Cotswolds only in summer. This limestone, gravelly country dries up quickly after rain. Autumns bring the splendour of the beechwoods. Winters are cold, rough and bright, for south-west winds clear the sky as quickly as they darken it; in winter, too, when trees are bare, the shape of the wolds shows up most strongly. And spring's daffodils at the Eastleaches, Coln St Aldwyns or a dozen other places are a sight incomparable. You can get a night's lodging at most hotels throughout the winter, at some till Christmas and from Easter, and prices then are low. As for a ploughman's lunch or midday snack, there are few Cotswold pubs where such cannot be bought round the year. We decided, therefore, to write this book for all seasons, so that, should you decide to take a week's holiday in autumn, winter or spring, you would have some idea of the pleasures in store for you. We ourselves drafted the first chapter in mid-March, the last in early December.

This book is, as its title says, an introduction. Of the many books that can tell you more, we suggest two: *The Cotswolds: a New Study* (David & Charles), which we edited, and which contains studies of the Cotswolds past and present, by many recognised experts; and David Verey's *Gloucestershire: The Cotswolds* (Penguin Books), a delightfully written guide to Cotswold buildings. We also wrote *The Cotswolds* (Batsford, 1966). It has been out of print for some years. This new book has given us the happiness of revisiting every town, village, almost every hamlet. Occasionally we have used a sentence or two from the old book, where we felt the strength of the old Quaker advice: 'beware of making additions . . . when it was well left before'. Otherwise all the material is newly gathered and arranged.

One final point, though we are sure it will not apply to you, gentle reader. Cotswolds people are friendly and welcoming: they will willingly guide and help you. In return, remember that what is for some a tourist area is for them their home and workplace. Therefore keep to roads, public footpaths and common land, and off farms; and when you stop, park your car and walk about or picnic with thought for those to whom the Cotswolds are their home. Then, not only will you be welcomed, but when you leave, people will say as to their friends: 'Please come back soon'.

Down Burford Way

We began at Burford, in March, at dusk. We settled in at the Bay
Tree Hotel, ate, and with winter coats on stepped out into
Sheep Street, under a brilliant ceiling of stars just above our
heads. Orion and the Plough were almost within our hands
from the old stone doorway. We walked along to the High
Street and down towards the Windrush bridge. Dark entrances
under old stone arches led to lighted courts or windows, pub
doors, window-boxes, tubs of bulbs. On one side of the old
narrow bridge the mill-stream was foaming creamy over a weir
into tumbled water lit by a house window. On the other, the
river stream ran quiet and dark, under bushes in the field.

The church spire rose up pale and clear against the dark
brilliant sky. Lighted windows of a small school in the square
showed young ones shouting and squealing as they went to bed
in rooms papered with youthful art. In the churchyard, row
behind row of carved tombs and stones glimmered faint and
intricate in the school window light. The spire touched the
handle of the Plough above.

Next morning I looked out early on old dark roofs half green
with moss, gold-grey walls, March boughs with the hint of
coming green, faint sky with light behind the mist, and heard
birds everywhere. Out and about the town after breakfast, increasing sun brought out the stone's gold, and the schoolkids.
Shops were opening, baskets of fresh broccoli and celery arriv-
ing, vans rattling round corners and, of course, men were digging up the road. Burford has no central market-place like
Cirencester, Fairford, Northleach or Minchinhampton, but
instead a wide main street, like Chipping Campden or
Moreton-in-Marsh. I looked up the long slope of the High
Street rising between green verges and lime trees to the top of
the wold, every building enticing and delighting the eye with
rich, strict, subtle beauty. Not one broke the rhythm and unity.

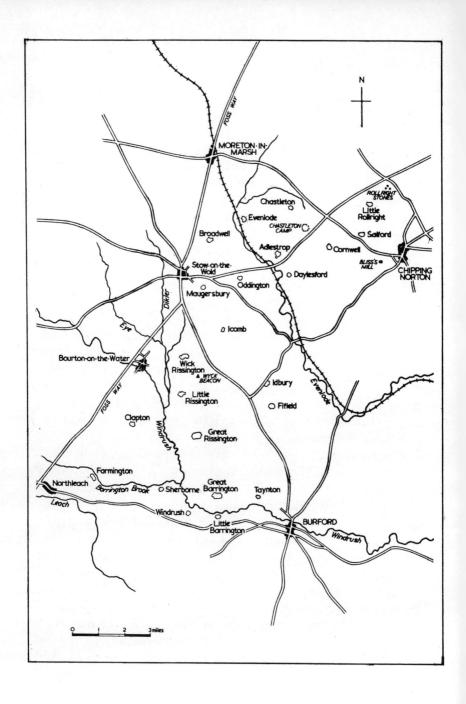

N

FOSS WAY

MORETON-IN-
MARSH

ROLLRIGHT
STONES

Chastleton

Little
Rollright

Evenlode

CHASTLETON
CAMP

Salford

Broadwell

Adlestrop

Cornwell

BLISS'S
MILL

CHIPPING
NORTON

Stow-on-the-
Wold

Daylesford

Dikler

Maugersbury

Oddington

Eye

Icomb

Bourton-on-the-Water

Wick
Rissington

WYCK
BEACON

Idbury

Evenlode

FOSS WAY

Little
Rissington

Fifield

Windrush

Clapton

Great
Rissington

Farmington

Great
Barrington

Taynton

Northleach

Barrington Brook

Sherborne

Leach

Windrush

Little
Barrington

BURFORD

Windrush

0   1   2   3 miles

Looking the other way, down to the river and the bridge, there was the same incredible standard of style and achievement, houses clustered more thickly in the village's little centre, the church spire rising behind. Over the bridge rose the background of the wolds. The bridge has not been widened for traffic, which keeps down the number of cars pouring through the place, and the speed at which they come.

Burford on the Windrush river, in the east Cotswolds, has been a busy country village for a thousand years. Wychwood forest once spread round it, three thousand acres of wild land and woodland, haunt of witches, enchantments, brigands and homeless men, deer, timber and sport. Now, though greatly reduced, it is a national nature reserve. The church as we see it had been built by 1400. The almshouses given by Warwick the Kingmaker, the grammar school near them, the sturdy pillared Tolsey for market and town business in the High Street, were all there by the 1570s.

In the fifteenth, sixteenth and seventeenth centuries, as English life expanded and stone was found in quantities in this area, people rebuilt their mainly timber houses and shops in it, from the local quarries. The high quality of this area's stone developed possibilities and a discipline which masons obeyed. The result was greater than they knew. During those centuries the High Street and its immediate branches were built almost as they are today, big and small houses closely neighbouring each other, each one differing by its builder's individuality, all harmonising in disciplined style and in the warm stone and dark tiles common to this soil. Here is a grinning face, a canopy to a porch, a bird in a cluster of leaves carved by a door. There are bookshops, many crafts and antiques, streets leading to walks between hedges and by the Windrush. *The Countryman* is published from a sixteenth-century house in Sheep Street, which was formerly the *Greyhound* inn and still has greyhounds on its gateposts.

Every trader packed his front premises into High Street. Some, like London House and Castle's, show their long ancestry. Thriving men built houses in little Sheep Street, Witney Street, Swan Lane, or down towards the river in Priory

Lane near the old priory. The industrial revolution by-passed the Cotswolds. Then, a hundred years ago, the social reformer and craftsman William Morris began to make people aware of the values that were waiting to be rediscovered there, especially at Burford and Chipping Campden. A pair of Burford people, the Grettons, examined the history of every village trade family, street, old building and yard in the town. This encouraged people to strip and expose ancient shop-fronts, cellars, attics and courts, thereby preserving a historic Burford character in the modern town. Feeling has continued strong enough to keep developments within the native tradition.

The Burford and District Society leads tours of one hour round the town every Sunday at 3 pm from the Tolsey. These can take you into private grounds, houses or mason's premises, and give you a taste of the pure spring, the small beer and good wine of the place.

We took the country road over Burford bridge and up the wolds to Taynton. Behind us from Little Fulbrook the whole beauty of Burford spread beside its stream and up the long slope opposite. It was no dream, but real life in our own time. The eastern wolds opened out as we went on, tractors with disc harrows breaking light-brown soil, copses still winter-dark.

Taynton and the two Barringtons were the homes of great masons in the building of this famous stone country. Little Taynton's quiet street shows a native distinction in its steep roofs, gently angled corners, windows with stone mullions and delicate drip-moulds, and its stone tiles that hold deep shades of colour. Jackdaws were busy stuffing straw into the handsome chimneys. A proper farm-yard on the village street was clearly their supply store. From the slope one looks down on the finest show of Cotswold roofs and tiling skill one could find packed into a little area. Some are new, some centuries old, but one can hardly tell which, so perfectly does the stone suit its background and hold its colour as it mellows.

This stone has bred generations of skilled masons like the Kempsters, the Strongs and many others whose names are cut on village tombstones round here. Thomas and Edward Strong were leading builders of St Paul's Cathedral, by Sir Christopher

14

Wren's appointment. Taynton stone was built into Blenheim Palace, Merton College, Oxford and St George's Chapel, Windsor. Taynton church is the most delightful, simple place. Those corbelled faces must have been portraits of the capable women and shrewd men the sculptors knew, so vivid are the personalities. All the windows are different, the capitals of the short sturdy pillars are different, steps go up to nowhere, the bosses on the little roof are bright with gold. Coming out of its stillness, the spring birds and sunshine gave me a pang of pleasure. Late snowdrops were thick round old, ornamented tombs.

The two Barringtons, Great and Little, lie on opposite sides of the Windrush, rather lonesome, even odd. At Great Barrington the smith told me his father and grandfather had worked the forge, and that his relations were smiths, bakers, post office and shop-keepers throughout the Cotswolds. He had plenty of work, welding and repairing machines as well as blacksmith's work. In his forge, its smith-coal furnace stacked ready for use, the rows of tools stood like soldiers, all fashioned for a purpose and all individual. Smiths are in demand again, for this kind of work and because of the growing passion for ponies and horses.

The *Fox* inn, half-way to Little Barrington, is a proper country pub in an idyllic situation with arms of the Windrush on either side and huge trees for a frame. It is a Donnington house, serving the beer of the last independent brewery in the Cotswolds (see p. 84), whose 'real ale' is always worth seeking out. Little Barrington cottages are ranged on banks above road and river. No-one was about, but a white gander and his grey goose on the green slope watched us closely. A small barn has a dignified tiled porch, a cottage row an old stone arch in the middle leading to gardens. A traditional group stands round the church, the home farm laid out in a hollow, with well kept buildings and modern machines. The little church is wholly of its countryside, with a long stone seat outside for those who like the feel of the church but can't face going in, tea-caddy and table tombs with moss and snowdrops and primroses. We went back through the village, which was too much for the gander,

15

who ran hissing and wing-beating after us, applauded by the goose.

Along the shaded green Windrush valley to Windrush village the sun was catching clean ploughland, hazy tree-tops, and the bare grazing-line of the wolds. We watched young Friesians grazing. Two horse-trailers passed us, each showing two rugged-up, tail-bound rears. As the road rose along the wold's side, the river shore twinkled from below through bare branches.

Windrush village clings to a steep slope. The course of the river, east-west so far, here turns north towards its distant source near Snowshill. Grouped on a steep bend, roofs, gables, dormer windows and chimneys make a pattern of beauty strong through the necessities of their situation. Richard Toombes cut his name on his little porch here in 1688.

The church and churchyard are well known. Here are magnificent tombs topped with rolls like bales of wool, as at Burford; in one, the fluting in the hollowed ends of the bale is half turning into the mask of a ram's head. Strange energy was working here in the 1100s. The hands that carved the holy entrance porch cut guilty creatures with human/animal heads and great beaks or beards. Inside, the door being shut on them, the church recovers humanity and Christ, local and lovely. One corbel has a ram's head, and on the next arch, is it a mouse?

We went on along the country road to Sherborne that lies on the Windrush's small tributary, the Sherborne brook. This country has a subtle difference. The life of small farms, simple effects of cottage and cowsheds, difficulties of mud, fallen trees, toil of mending stone walls and shed roofs, rises here into an art, an achievement. The land is farmed with authority and scope. Sherborne village was looking idyllic in spring sunshine, a pear orchard breaking into buds and a flock of white-faced Border Leicester sheep grazing beneath them. Estate cottages, built in groups, suggest more interior space than is usual. The whole valley is open parkland, with the Sherborne brook running down the middle. A fall in the brook and a tiny 7-arched footbridge gently centres the whole landscape.

Sherborne House, in existence since 1551, has been enlarged

and altered. It now holds the International Academy for Continuous Education. Joined to it by a passage is the little church, a tempered, reflective building, perhaps weighing up the odds against anything better after death than had been achieved in life and ended here. There are monuments by the great sculptors of their age, Rysbrack and Westmacott, and a memorial to the young Princess Bariatinsky, which I enjoyed for the social-historical scene of 1806-7 which it presented.

For two miles, from Sherborne along the brook to Farmington, you can see the Cotswold country almost without a building. Old lichened roofs of a field cowshed look like mossy caves. The brook gleams through the roadside copses. When I was last in Farmington, the dovecote in the stable-yard of the big house, open to the road, was in a miserable state, holes in the round wall, roof tiles fallen and timber gone. This March when I came to the yard entrance, the circular wall and roof, the tiny round lantern had been returned to perfection. Time had run back and here was a little age of gold. On the green, is a small octagonal pump house, restored by the people of Farmington, Connecticut, USA.

From Farmington we cut across lonesome country between 500 and 700ft up to Clapton – and how rewarding a journey it was! The land here is rich, almost lavish, by Cotswold's sparse soil standards. Yellowish winter grass is often replaced by the full green of leys (fields of specially planted grass). Winter crops were up in six inches of brilliant green. Young beeches gave promise of two hundred years of beauty. There was pleasure in the solitary journey, in untrimmed verges, walls often broken and tangled with last September's creepers, clumps of rough bushy shelter for birds. On the left, superb views of wolds and colours unrolled towards the Guitings and Roel Hill. Ahead the land went up, up to nothing but sky. Every dip swung the road up to another rise. On the turn to Clapton I saw hedges properly 'laid', where the tall shoots are slashed low down, not cut through, and laid sideways on the hedge, so that along their length the buds send up new shoots for the next layer. Stakes hold the shape together. Thus a dense hedge is made, instead of an uneven one with tall tufts. The

17

road still climbed. Stony fields now, lines of over-grown red cabbage in one, and suddenly we were on the crest, where the upper valley of the Windrush spreads out across to the Rissingtons.

Up here is Clapton, a tiny group of cottages with gabled manor house and church to scale; miles of unbuilt distances, and clear sweet air that seems to take all the heaviness out of you. Within the churchyard (whose gate is made of horseshoes by a local man) a new beech has been planted among daffodils. A clothes-line over the wall looked cheerful with dancing, scarlet jeans. The church is most delightful, welcoming, indefinably gay. Its east window is just a bright coloured slit; side windows of clear glass let in the sun and the familiar village scene, while an angel in the beam above the tiny altar smiles as you approach. Everything is devotedly polished and cared for.

I wanted to see again the old bridge called New Bridge over the Windrush. We had to get down from 700ft, and a turning marked 'Unsuitable for Motors' looked just the thing. So it was. The lane dived between heavy wet plough, winter cabbage, winter wheat, rounded a bend and got wetter and narrower, trees touched overhead, birds almost collided, field grass turned into bristly clumps in marsh, the road flattened, and there was the river and the old New Bridge. I assured myself that it was still drowsing in its hidden world known only to hedgers, anglers and lovers, and listened to the lipping of clean, fast, shallow water.

To get to Bourton-on-the-Water one crosses a land full of springs and brooks. Indeed, Bourton is very much on the water, though the shaggy wild wet rural world is put in order on the approaches to the village. A notice for TEAS was welcome. The construction of many new houses (all faced with reconstituted stone, see p. 49), none of them empty, is proof of Bourton's attraction. Most visitors only know its summer face, thick traffic, country crowds, countless amusements. But Bourton has a whole personality and a long history.

The river Windrush flows through the middle of the little place, between broad green verges under the graceful, low, stone foot-bridges for which Bourton is famous. They were built between 1756 and 1953, though Bourton Bridge (1806) on the Foss Way stands where the Romans first built a bridge, and the English another in 1483. You can see seventeenth-century cottages in Victoria Street, a corn-mill and cottages in Sherborne Street, and many fine, plain, early nineteenth-century houses in Moore Street.

Bourton is a country-outing place, not a sophisticated tour stop. It has everything for country visitors: beautiful buildings, plenty of refreshments, a model village, an aquarium, witches, a model railway exhibition, grass strips by the river for picnics and play and rest for the feet, and best of all, 'Birdland', the devoted work of a local man. I like to see the Midland Farmers' big building of cheerful blue and floury dust right in the middle of the scrum, the old millstream, millhouse and dovecote behind the *Duke of Wellington*, and the flowering trees all down that green and golden street by the river.

Bourton has its own life quite apart from the visitors' trade. Music, crafts, sports and schools go on all the year. An unusual craft is church embroidery. A distinguished embroiderer with some pupils produces here the altar frontals and clergy vestments which may become historic treasures as the centuries roll by – such as you see in Winchcombe, Chipping Campden and Cirencester. Many go overseas. The kneelers and festal pieces in Bourton church are her group's work.

It was here that I first saw a new kind of artificial roof tile. Tiling is always the weak point of even the best new building. These tiles were different, being thick and rough like stone, of a strong colour, properly graduated in sizes up the roof. If we cannot all have real stone slates at a price we can afford, I welcome such good artificial ones as these, while hoping that people who can afford to do so will continue to use the real ones.

A crow would say that from Bourton to Wick Rissington is a mile and a half, across the Dikler brook. But we went past the new Bourton school to the Roman Foss Way, to see what is left of Bourton station on the old Cheltenham & Banbury Direct railway over the Cotswolds that opened in 1881. A building, a platform and canopy still remain. We turned on to the Foss

19

Way to cross the little river Eye, then right again over the Dikler and, immediately afterwards, the old railway bridge. It is now an antiquity, in true line of succession from the Roman road.

The three Rissington villages lie south from here, a mile or so from each other. Wick Rissington lies across a common, with scattered cottages, a village pond, Muscovy ducks and a lovely view over the river valley to a gentle rise of many-coloured fields. Thick clumps of snowdrops patched the hedges still in March. The hamlet is very small and stone-built. In the south wall of the church is a window said to represent a total eclipse of the sun in 1322. The green colour in it is striking. Gustav Holst was organist here as a young man in 1892, and also conductor of the choral society orchestra at Bourton-on-the-Water. Some years ago a vicar of Wick Rissington had a vision, directing him to make a maze 500yd long round a certain big tree in the vicarage garden, to symbolise the progress of the Christian life. Unlike you and me, he took the vision seriously, and did exactly as he had been directed. You can follow it, as I did.

Little and Great Rissington are south of Wick, all three just over a mile from each other by path. It is worth going up Wyck Beacon on the way, 800ft high and with a prehistoric round barrow, to see the Cotswold country spread wide and high and coloured. Drop down then to Little Rissington, a village built against bleak winters and loneliness. Neat, straight-up cottages make a snaky narrow street that gets down off the exposed hillside as fast as possible. The houses are all pretty, gabled, with stone roofs, proper Cotswold chimneys, many stone-mullioned windows. Clusters of old houses, stables and one or two new houses stand back from the winding street.

The church is built on a green rise at the end of the village. Part of the churchyard holds the graves of men from the RAF Central Flying School at Great Rissington, killed on service. The churchyard looks west over the Windrush, over Bourton, over miles of wolds and a huge spread of airmen's sky. Looking the other way, you get one of the best views of the village. The church is small and charmingly home-made, with every stocky pillar having a different decoration.

Great Rissington is 'great' by the possession of the only primary school and the only pub in the three villages. The houses climb uphill, rather scattered. There is a beautiful farmhouse at the beginning of the rise and a proper, well kept animal and farm background to the village. High banks to the road carry cottage gardens with cabbages, purple-sprouting broccoli, rhubarb. On a triangle at the top of the village, just where one stops and turns to see the view, is the *Lamb*, well sited.

Then we went out onto the high wolds at 700ft, roll after roll in the wind and sun, plough, stone walls and partridges – and there was the great aerodrome, listed for closure as we write. A gun-post marked the entrance, but we drove past, saw the land shaved flat for learner pilots, the end of the runway close to the road, and read the famous RAF names to the camp roads.

We cut across the A424 to Icomb, all the way on the 700ft contour line, and then climbed Icomb hill. Clouds had come up thick and dark behind, while the spread of wolds in front was bright with sun. There is an Iron Age fort on the top, a good lookout by Cotswold dwellers watching for raiders coming across the easy midland country. Ragged firs mark the crown of the hill across a field of turnip. Suddenly the land was extinguished in shadow, and bright light streamed from behind the cloud through a curtain of rain.

Down the hill road to Icomb village. Handsome houses set among well planted trees dot the valley slopes, tractors were out pulling disc harrows over ploughland, and Icomb was a nest of dark roofs, warm stone walls and grey chimneys, set in oaks and ash, close and pretty in its separateness. So quiet, so old and real. A village pump was the first thing I saw, with a lamp. There are seventeenth- and eighteenth-century cottages, and Icomb Place, *rebuilt* about 1420. And if you want to see the man who rebuilt it then, look at the effigy in the church of Sir John Blaket, made in 1431. Along the side are his relations.

I entered the church past a nice cowshed, full of brown and white rumps and tails. Inside the church I read a list of vicars or patrons, the first appointed in 1240, and knew I really was in old England. The communion-rail step was covered by three

21

kneelers. On them were worked in needlework the words, the stave and the melody notes of 'The heavens are telling the glory of God', 'Let their celestial concerts all unite', and 'Let all the world in every corner sing', and the dedication, 'In happy memory of Ruth Moss Music Maker'. Not only as a choral singer myself, but as part of old England in modern England, I gave thanks.

I came out into warm air and a wonderful smell of cow. A man in the yard carrying a couple of empty buckets waved to me. Snowdrops, but also Whitsuntide bosses, lit the graves. The afternoon sun and quiet flowed over the eastern wolds down across the Evenlode, lighting every undulation of the land, every shade of the greening twigs.

A curious, little-known area lies east of Stow-on-the-Wold, stretching to Chipping Norton at the extremity of the real Cotswolds on the slope down into Oxfordshire. Here are Oddington, Daylesford, Cornwell, Adlestrop, Broadwell, Evenlode, Chastleton, Salford. This was Wychwood country, very quiet and with its own secrets.

From Icomb we went across country to Oddington, a little place of beautiful Cotswold buildings, some very old, with cottage terraces and interesting conversions of farm buildings. I saw a pedigree herd grazing, each cow wearing her collar, and a stable-yard with heads at a dozen half-doors. The village moved bodily at some period. The abandoned church is now restored and has many rare survivals, well worth seeking out. Nearby Daylesford and Adlestrop are confusing, because the winding roads go round them both and you don't know which one you are seeing at any moment – a Wychwood effect, in and out, reel and rout.

Daylesford was the home of the great Warren Hastings, administrator and reformer in the East India Company in the eighteenth century. In the churchyard is Hastings' tomb, grave and simple after such greatness, pain and malice. On the stone urn is carved only 'Warren Hastings 1818'.

The Adlestrop station of Edward Thomas' poem has gone, though the Oxford & Worcester line is open. If Thomas had also seen the Adlestrop post office, with its round roof thatched, telephone-box built into it and thatched too, he would have written another poem.

On then to Cornwell, a place wishing to be unknown. It is a charming hamlet in beautiful condition, with shop and post office, village hall, water-splash, washing lines, kids' playground, church and big house, but we had to be persevering to see it. 'Private Road' met us on both sides, the shop is only opened at particular hours, and the church, which takes a deal of finding, is locked with no instruction where to get the key.

This countryside holds many secrets, from which old stories and power-invoking rhymes have grown. Cornwell has a set of stone circles, and the Rollright stones themselves stand only three or four miles on, north-west of Chipping Norton on the cold hill-side. Here is the single King stone, the weird circle of twisted stones round which the air carries whispers for those who can hear, and the five traitor-knights' stones.

Chipping Norton, three miles from the stones, is an open, windy place, lively and busy. It was crowded with cars and local people when we arrived. The prefix 'Chipping' means market. The town centre is on two levels, and runs up to the *Blue Boar* and the *Crown & Cushion*. You can see that Chipping Norton is not a village grown big, but a small town, no doubt due to the 'chipping'. There is a feeling for town houses here, not only cottages. The little town hall is on the lower level, and the guildhall, with pillars, on the upper. The main streets are all of stone, and old stone archways give glimpses of older nooks and privacies. The *Blue Boar*, so named in 1683, is the original inn of the town and was a hospice run by nuns for travellers in the Middle Ages, needed in this lonely upland region. The bar inside is charmingly thatched, and sells a local beer brewed at Hook Norton, off the Cotswolds but not far.

Church Street, dropping down from the centre and giving long views over wooded country, has eight gabled almshouses with a stone arch, eight front doors and nine chimneys. Spring Street is the kind of street I love, with a raised pavement protecting the houses, domestic, snug, looking like proper home life. A new small theatre is being built here, to serve every need that a

23

busy town and countryside can put it to.

Chipping Norton church is one of the big Cotswold 'wool' churches, meaning those which owe much of their size and beauty to wealth earned from the wool trade. Its splendid porch was built in the sixteenth century. 'The story says that a priest chased five devils out of the church, then hunted them up to the market place and into a flock of sheep. In the vaulted ceiling of the porch you can see the five horrible faces. They come no further. The nave and aisles and choir are dwellings of light, grace and spirit. Here too is the window in the eastern wall of the nave, above the chancel roof, a characteristic of the wool churches of Cirencester, Chipping Campden, Northleach and Fairford. An interesting window on the east wall of the south aisle contains panes of shooting stars, storks, fish, elephants and giraffe.

Half a mile out of Chipping Norton on the A44, you see· down the valley a most unusual-looking mill. It is laid out in a rectangle, towers at each corner, a dome in the middle and, rising from the dome, a tall chimney-stack. The mill front has an ornamental stone facing. A millpond at one side is fed by the valley stream. This is Bliss's mill, which was established in 1746.

The managing director passed me on to the works engineer who took me round. Bliss's mill is not just a means of earning a living or producing cloth, but a real entity. Workers spoke and smiled as we went past the up-to-date machines. When I enquired about the chimney-stack and the former steam-engine, I found no favourite aunt could have been spoken of more regretfully.

'It's the quality of our cloth that has kept us up,' said the engineer in his soft local voice. 'If we had tried to compete with the mass-produced stuff of some mills we'd have been out of business years ago. As it is, we've all the work that we can do, because of our quality. More than 60 per cent of our stuff goes for export. You see, we're a private firm, no-one to say we must do it this way or that. We can keep up our quality.' I said that I thought textiles had not been trouble-makers in English industries. One did not read of strikes. 'Strikes?' he exclaimed.

24

'We haven't had a strike since – let me see – 1926! *That* was connected with the General Strike.'

Two miles on we came to Salford, a tiny upland village off the main road. I remember this day in a shaft of sunlight because of Salford's *Black Horse*, where we had lunch. The *Black Horse* had a couple of locals in, one in gumboots, one in a suit, and did us good bread and cheese and pickles. A photograph of Salford celebrations on VJ day showed us everyone in the village. Pictures of the activities of the Stirrers Uppers' Club stirring up village life made us twitch slightly. Male singing sounded outside. The locals said 'Trouble coming. Steptoe and Son'. A couple of cheerful, ordinary fellows came in, and for the rest of our lunch we enjoyed a serial tossed to and fro in soft Cotswold voices about a donkey who got a parking ticket, and joined the local hunt and got 'geed up'.

From this happy moment we took the A44 towards Moreton-in-Marsh, making for Chastleton House and hill. We passed the big Cross Hands quarry of building stone, and turned off to Chastleton House. Ploughland here was full of small stones, hedges were properly laid, thatchers were at work on village roofs. Some 200ft below the hilltop camp, Chastleton House is a big five-gabled building which was built about 1603-10. Almost unaltered, it has many relics of King Charles I and a box topiary garden. Chastleton House is open all round the year except on Wednesdays.

The dominating hill-top drew us, like Icomb a Cotswold watch-point over the raiders' routes. From the road at 700ft, where nothing is to be seen but patchy fields of thin grass, far-off farm roofs and copses of trees, the track goes up to the green mound circle of the fort, thickly overgrown with trees and bushes. Rough stone work was visible at the gap made for cows, and among tangled hawthorn roots. A lean-to shed and some cows were in the muddy centre. I have been up here in June when the flat centre is an unbroken lake of green wheat and the mound a scented castle well of dog-roses – but beauty made no difference to the alien chill, the sense of a life not yours, of presences waiting for you to go. This time again the camp was preoccupied with itself, with the larks' shrill bodiless song, the

25

archaic cattle, with the huge depths of air and sky, and the inhuman forbidding mud.

Swinging west now to the homeward Burford run, Evenlode, Broadwell and Maugersbury lie ahead, and then by-roads to Idbury and Fifield. The Evenlode rises above Moreton-in-Marsh. The village lies a little up from its river, a screened and gentle spot in as quiet a valley as you could find in south England.

Down the road, over the Oxford-Worcester railway, over the Evenlode, and the road rises to my favourite unknown village, Broadwell. It is such a pretty, open place and looks cheerful in any weather. Cotswold villages are usually grouped and planted for shelter – open ones are hardy and look it. Broadwell has a big green with houses dotted round and a brook on one side making a little ford, sheep grazing, and the *Fox* pub. A blacksmith's shop stands on the green opposite the pub. We saw beehives too, a nice little bus shelter, lots of new stone walling and the entrance to a splendid manor house of the eighteenth century. A Roman site lies behind. There are other good houses, some of them seventeenth-century farmhouses, but, sadly, the old stone slates of some have been replaced by ugly mud-coloured artificial tiles.

The church is very attractive, old, with modern work in glass and tower screen. A memorial speaks of Peter Thursby who was present with his father at the siege of Lucknow. They must have had stories to tell during winter evenings in Broadwell. The churchyard has a mighty old yew of memorable girth and vigour, and more of those fine seventeenth-century tombs with wool-bale tops. Coloured primroses had run wild, and I was glad to see graves left as green mounds in their individual shape and not flattened to help the mower.

Young trees are being planted all over the Cotswolds, and in Broadwell I saw some young yews, bringing a very happy feeling of continuity from century to century. Arthur Gibbs, writing *A Cotswold Village* late in the nineteenth century, when his beloved native villages were decaying under the disastrous results of long agricultural depression, feared that in a hundred years' time the people would all have gone and the villages would be rotting shells. He could not foresee the prosperity that was to come, through State support of farming by deficiency payments and grants, nor how money made in industry was to pour into the countryside after 1945, followed by an increasing number of people.

Maugersbury is a mile up-hill towards Stow, a little settlement with a manor house built in the sixteenth century, and six farmhouses of the seventeenth, all of the proper Cotswold architecture, one with its board up: 'The Oxlease Herd of British Friesians'.

We went along the Stow-Burford road for four miles and then turned off to Idbury and Fifield. Woods warm the road into Stow, but after the junction with the Foss Way it runs on towards Burford, open and lonely. In late afternoons when the sun is down towards the top of the high wolds on your right, a wonderful light bathes the landscape ahead and the Evenlode valley on the left. The Cotswolds are not only the villages, farms and buildings. They are the wolds, and valleys, the light limestone soil that grows fresh, pale-tinted plants of barley, upland grass, milk-white hawthorn, translucent green leaves of beech, grey-green sprays of willow. The wolds swell and dip gently, with no eye-catching formations, but a marvellous, subtle, ever-varying form pointed faintly by combes with little springs, or patches of old quarries. Their effect is always to lead your gaze to the sky, the faint blue, hazy or bright-clouded sky, always changing with the south-west wind.

Behind Rissington airfield, flocks of crows and gulls were following tractors. Idbury fort is in the middle of plough, a green circle in old trees, with countless birds swooping over it. Idbury itself has some sensitive new building. Up here, too, I saw an old-fashioned object which is not completely confined to the pages of Thomas Hardy and country novelists – a lambing pen, up on a bare wold in the wind. It was an enclosure of about 30 by 20yd, made of bales of straw. All round the outer wall of bales ran a narrow passage, thatched over at about 4ft in height, with hurdle partitions and openings into the central space. The passage, or maternity ward, was dark, snug and safe from wind. I could hear mothers and new lambs baa-ing and bleating. In the middle were feeding places for other sheep with lambs. A clothes-prop stuck in a hurdle in the middle carried a lantern. Outside the pen the field was full of sheep and lambs. Idbury Manor used to be the publishing house of *The Countryman*, and was then the centre for a *Look and Learn* course of cooking and food presentation. Unusual and high quality recipes, many local, have been collected from this into the *Idbury Cook Book*.

Fifield is poised on a rise between the Evenlode and Windrush valleys. It is a rectangular village, rather bleak but handsome. Thence a by-road runs for four miles, skirting only farms, to rejoin the main road a mile from Burford. These are very fine farms, Hill Farm with a steam engine in the yard, High Lodge Farm, Springhill Farm where you can see the Cotswold roofs of tiny Upper Milton and smell the friendly pig. We passed old quarries, the gold of the country, at Blackheath Clump and were back in sheep country instead of plough. We saw the Windrush valley and the warm roofs of Burford, the smoke from its chimneys, the church spire, and so returned to a big fire and a good supper. After that, anyone would feel adventurous enough to stroll out in the quiet, see the gabled silhouettes against the stars, drop in to the *Bull* for a port and lemon near the fire among young folk of all kinds, or to the *Mermaid*, where you can read magazines with your drink, or to tread the white stone flags of the *Lamb* bar, old and comfortable, burning long logs in an open hearth.

The tour described in this chapter falls within OS 1:50,000 maps No 163 (Cheltenham and Cirencester) and 164 (Oxford)

Leach, Coln and Water Park

The main Cotswold streams are the Windrush, Evenlode, Isbourne and Dikler in the centre north, with the smaller Barrington brook, Knee brook and River Eye; the Coln, Leach and Churn, with the Ampney brook in the centre; the Frome, Avon and many small streams round Nailsworth in the south. The limey and gravelly soil delights in throwing up winter-bournes or springs that support streams only in rainy seasons, so that one can often find more brooks than are in any list.

The Leach glides through country which has no thought of the world. It is known for Northleach church, twin Eastleaches, and summer water happiness by the river at Lechlade. The stream rises just south-east of the Foss Way near Hampnett beyond Northleach. There is no road along it, which makes its finding your own effort, and much wilder.

We set out from Burford on the Northleach road to follow the middle Leach, making for Aldsworth. The morning was brisk and bright up on the A40, with mist on the further wolds and in the furrows of some ploughland. A track between plough to the left tempted us to Camp Barn, another prehistoric fort and village site. You can walk round the top of the mound, see the old stones in the turf. Behind you, north, the land falls to the Windrush valley. In front, south, you can see Cricklade and the White Horse Downs in Oxfordshire, with Cirencester tucked in to the west.

A touch of humanity in farming was given by the family sight of a short, square red bull with two short, square red cows and two shorter, square red calves. As we turned off the A40 the stone walls came back, chequering the land. Aldsworth is known for the Garnes, farmer breeders who maintained the only surviving flock of Old Cotswold sheep, until the revival of concern for old breeds. Those interested can now see these sheep at the Cotswold Farm Park at Bemborough (p. 80). But

29

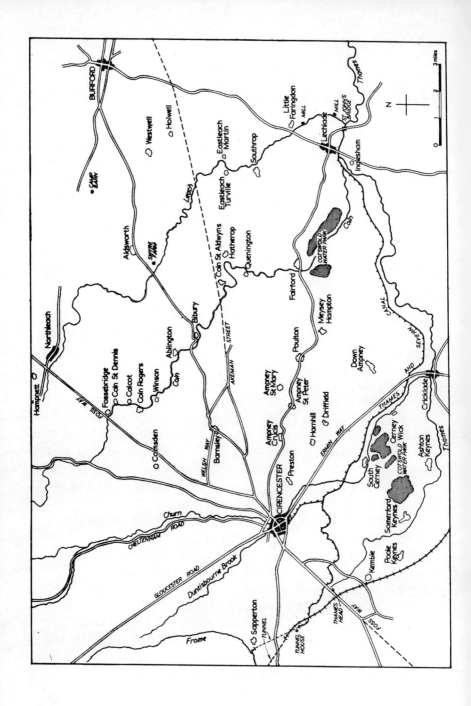

the big flock that I saw scattered over the high wold leading into Aldsworth were haughty, Roman-nosed Border Leicesters with their lambs.

This is a cheerful, hillside village facing the morning sun. It stands steeply above the road, low stone street walls showing us the cottage daffodils, wallflowers, rhubarb and broccoli. Women were out polishing windows, and waved as we walked by. Piles of creamy stone lay in the sun on a corner, and a tractor and manure cart rumbled by. The old primary school, stone, with tall windows, was still doing its job, TV on the roof, nutty nibbles for the tits on the low boughs, and kids chasing each other in the playground.

Down in the green sunny dip was a tiny tributary of the Leach. A pretty woman washing the porch step of her cottage that had 'William Mary, 1728' cut over the door, told me that her cottage had once been a little school. Stepping across the brook by a stone, I went up the mossy churchyard path to the church, an old favourite of unpriced, simple joys. I could not but smile at the book of Register of Marriages. The first entry was for December 1823-4, and 1974 came only half-way through. The book should last until 2125, or thereabouts.

Now we took a remote, roaming way to Akeman Street and the Eastleaches, via Swyre Farm, the entrance to Dean Farm, and Williamstrip Farm. At Swyre the Leach is 4ft wide at flood time, in clean rolling country all ploughland (often stony) and stone walls, pointed by superb barns. Past the handsome Williamstrip Farm, we turned left into Roman Akeman Street, a tall hedge on the south side and open land to the north.

Here you are on the Macaroni land, with Macaroni Downs Farm to the north and Macaroni Farm to the south (Macaronis were eighteenth-century exquisites who copied Continental fashions, but why here?) And now our pursuit of the Leach showed us the best house conversion in all this area. The country is steep here, great clumps of smooth-trunked beeches, low, old walls each side of Akeman Street. Coming out of one clump, I found an old farm complex called Sheephill Barn now singularly transformed into – what shall I call it – a modern seeing of the Roman villa, a setting for a full, cultivated rural life. The barn with its huge porch was restored to its prime, and adapted to domestic living; the long line of cowsheds leading from it was opened up to reveal eleven stone pillars, stone bases and cut capitals, making a south-west cloister-walk for refreshment, thought or conversation. It led to a restored, tall, plain building, with wide cartway door and timber lintel, which commands a view of the most undisturbed and original fold of the Leach valley. There is no other house, only the sheep-walk valley sides, the deep confiding folds of the combe, the little stream, the seedling hawthorns, the slow-moving sheep.

As the road dropped down to the stream level, we turned aside from the Eastleach road to cross the Leach and see Westwell, not often sought out. It is a very still, beautiful place, where a banked stream feeds an old-fashioned pond. Let into the side of a huge block of stone set on two steps is a long narrow tongue of metal. This is a brass numeral from the clock of the shell-ruined Cloth Hall at Ypres, and forms part of a memorial to two men killed in the First World War. Low roofs, and a big house with trees cut like peacocks, carved animals on the gate and finials on the gables were reflected in the pond with the strange memorial. Moorhens searched for weed with the village ducks. The church was as old, unchanged and living as the little place. A memorial 300 years old showed fourteen children, boys with modern long hair, the girls' hair neatly plaited and pinned up.

Back to the country road to the Eastleaches. These are two tiny places with two churches, one each side of the stream, linked by a stone clapper bridge. Eastleach Turville is on a steep hillside, roads on two levels, beautiful houses and cottages on ledges, gardens spreading down banks, paths stepping down past an old spring house whose water was sought for its healing power, stone-tiled roofs here and there at foot level. A line of estate cottages with a clock tower makes a centre where all the paths meet. There is a very nice simple pub, the *Victoria*. The heart of the whole scene is the clear shining Leach, now 30ft wide, the clapper bridge, the green banks and the two old churches. Go in April when the stream banks are golden with

The central Cotswolds: *top* Spring near Ablington above the river Coln. Cotswold characteristics are clear: the dry stone walling, may in bloom, and beech clumps on a smooth skyline; *bottom* Hazleton, in high little-known country. The church, sixteenth-century Glebe House and farm make an unplanned group against chestnut and beech trees

The farming scene: *top* Summer and a harvested field near Frampton Mansell. Drystone walls mark the subtle folds, stone lies in the soil, may bushes and beech clumps break the light, buff colours; *bottom* The barn at Almsbury Farm near Winchcombe. Local skill laid the even courses of stone and the closely graded stone tiles on the roofs

daffodils, the willows and alders breaking into leaf, and the children lie on the bridge and fish with nets and jampots. It is all so miniature, and so real. Read the village notice board outside the Cotswold Stores 'up top' and see the 'Rummage Sale in aid of Whitsuntide Festivities'. You would want to be there!

The Keble family held the manor of Eastleach Turville from the sixteenth century, and John Keble, church reformer and poet, was curate of the two churches on his ordination in 1815 and, some say, built the clapper bridge. Four bellropes hang in St Martin's church. The bells must sound sweet across the meadow and stream, and echoing off the enclosing valley sides.

The Leach slips on past a mill, past the farming hamlet of Fyfield, to Southrop. It runs under the road at the village entrance, sparkling and clear under leaning willows, curves between low walls and under garden bridges, and then runs away across lonely country to its last two mills at Little Faringdon and Lechlade mill, and so into the Thames below St John's bridge.

Southrop village climbs gently up from the Leach level, a pretty street of stone houses and cottages, the road sunk with a raised pavement at gate level. A delightful school on the street, stone-tiled roof, stone chimney, TV, and teacher's bike in the little playground, seemed to combine old time values and new. A wonderful barn stands in the middle of the village, with gabled transepts, ventilating lantern, and pigeon-holes in rows along the whole upper part of one great wall. We reached the little church across the farm and stable-yard of a splendid manor house. Stone finials on house and farm put a delighting finish on the work. John Keble lived in the old vicarage, and gathered round him the men who set the Oxford Movement going in the Church of England.

Southrop has a large new building built near the green labelled 'Agricultural Merchants', which must contribute to the life of the place. A tennis club, two pubs, and some shops also help. We took the Leach-side road through Little Faringdon in order to approach Lechlade by St John's bridge and the *Trout* inn. We are here in river country, though

Cotswold too, because Leach and Coln fall into the Thames within a mile of one another, one each side of Lechlade. Land is level, roads are raised above it, deep flood-ditches lie on each side. Horses grazing, some wearing rugs, show good pasture, for the horse is a fussy feeder. 'Little Faringdon Stud' was posted over a big stable yard.

I was at school at Little Faringdon, the most notable thing I know about it. Miss Brownrigg was its mistress when I was five, so young that she had me to sleep in her bedroom. How I loved her! Since those days, I have discovered the ancient mill at Little Faringdon, just off the A361. Soon afterwards, we crossed the track of the Oxford-Fairford railway, which I used in wartime to get to Oxford from South Cerney for a day to see Charles whom I was going to marry, and the poet Charles Williams. It was very much a little line for romance and homely travellers.

We turned right on to the B4449, then into a field road to Lechlade mill and cottage, in a pretty river and island setting. And then away to St John's bridge, the Thames and the *Trout*.

St John's is one of the oldest stone bridges over the Thames. It was first built in 1229 by the prior of St John the Baptist's priory which stood where a caravan site and business is now situated. The *Trout* inn faces onto the road, but has water round it and grass down to trees and river. It caters for a great deal of business, but keeps the atmosphere we hoped to find – low timbers, trout and pike in glass cases, a river map, and a friendly face behind the bar.

We took our picnic lunch to the riverside by the bridge. Here is St John's lock, the first on the Thames, built in 1790. The lockkeeper was laying out a miniature house, pond, boat-house and rockery on the island. Boats at their moorings swayed gently beyond. The water reflected white cloud and new pale-blue paint on the lock. Blackthorn was out on the bank of the old stone bridge, young oak and wild rose budding. Across the green field, Lechlade houses were grouped round a tall slim spire.

Before going into Lechlade, it is worth making a short detour to visit Inglesham, in its watery maze. Take the by-road turn off the A417 south of St John's bridge, to Buscot Wick, follow it to

36

the A361, turn right and quickly left to Inglesham. You come along a track to a farmyard and a tiny church. On the other side of the farm is the young Thames, close beyond its farther banks the disused Thames & Severn Canal, and just beyond that, the river Coln. Both join the Thames here at Inglesham. The round-house, once the home of a canal lengthsman, is just through the willows.

In this silent plot of land is the tiny church at Inglesham, begun in the late 1100s. It is not only off the road, it is almost out of the world, so antique is it, and so small. The uneven stone floor, pale wooden pews, the dim roof, the heavy wooden bar on the north door make no place for dull eye or crude mind. Rather you could feel that the fire of thought and prayer, the vision of worker in stone and wood had concentrated through the centuries in the interior life which sustained them. A notice reads 'This church was repaired in 1888-9 through the energy and with the help of William Morris, who loved it.' When I came out, the sun was warm and cawing rooks sounded suddenly loud. Two fat pigeons were drinking out of a cow-trough.

By the road from Inglesham we came into Lechlade over the Ha'penny bridge, built about 1792, after the Thames & Severn Canal was opened. The house for collecting tolls still stands on the bridge. Beside it is the old wharf, now the premises of a busy boat-hiring firm, the old barge dock full of punts and skiffs. This was the highest point of regular navigation on the Thames. The river, of course, has always been a main artery from London across England to the west. Salt was brought by packhorse and cart from Droitwich, down the Salt Way across the Cotswolds to Lechlade for shipping to London. Corn and cheese went with it, and mixed goods came back.

Lechlade is therefore a very old settlement for trade, as well as for farming in its richly watered pastures. Its busy streets, all stone-built, show older occupations in arches big enough for waggons, or warehouses and stables now used for modern needs. The market place with the old *New Inn* and the sur-round of the church and three streets leading off it, makes a pretty centre with handsome, dignified houses and gardens.

The church is of the eleventh century and built of Taynton stone. Queen Katherine of Aragon once held the manor, and her sign, the pomegranate, is carved round the little door in the chancel. In Sherborne Street I saw a lorry full of fertiliser sacks from the Southrop firm. All along the banks of the Thames, Lechlade people enjoy the open grass meadows, the flowers and rushes of the winding water's edge, and the cheerful passing of pleasure boats, skiffs and canoes up and down. Buscot and Inglesham make good boating expeditions.

We had followed the line of the Leach to the Thames, and at Inglesham seen its neighbour stream, the Coln, also join the Thames. Now we set out to follow the Coln upstream to the Foss Way, where it changes character. The A417 took us the five miles from Lechlade to Fairford, past Lechlade houses which each have a little bridge across a stream to the road. Along the road one sees the gravel works, the dredging machinery, lorries, and the huge ponds with proprietary notices put up by angling, sailing, or country clubs. We came into Fairford past rather dull new housing, into the market place, a most charming and comfortable-looking mixture of street and square, with its bay-windowed *Bull Hotel*, set-back Fairford House, and famous little church. If you wander on, you come to the Coln again, and the town bridge, looking over parkland to a deep gabled seventeenth-century mill, with millrace and sluice and balustraded bridge. This is the beginning of a great trout-fishing stretch of the Coln. Go on over the bridge and turn left at Waterloo Lane for a river path which begins in interesting back gardens and leads on through fields and rough land for a real country walk.

Besides the market place there are two little centres, Milton End, several old houses facing a green, and East End, more haphazard, cottages with bands of unusual ornament, the *Eight Bells*, and some quiet village groups and corners. From the market place a stone arch leads through to a very pretty residential area.

The church, the steam fair, fishing and the new Cotswold Water Park are Fairford's main attractions. The church was rebuilt in the fifteenth century by John Tame, a wool and cloth merchant, particularly beautiful in itself and for its many delights in the topical carvings of choir seats, screens and roof corbels. Most of all it is famous for its windows. Just as many of our generation get their understanding from television rather than books, so John Tame planned to provide in his church a pictorial Bible and Christian schoolbook. The glass of the windows shows in continuity round the church the story of Christ's life from his birth to ascension: here you see the tall, brown Mount of Olives and Jesus' nail-scarred feet on the way up at the top of the window. The Last Judgement fills the west end. The artistic world importance of the glass lies in its all being of one period, roughly the reign of Henry VII (1485-1509), who owned the manor of Fairford and was building his chapel in Westminster Abbey and King's College, Cambridge. Almost certainly the king lent men from his school of glaziers. This was one of the advantages of having a good patron or lord of your manor. The happiest way to be acquainted with the church is to use it as it has been used for 500 years, go to a service, and watch the light through the windows, and the eight bellringers under the central tower, absorbed in their craft as they have been since these bells were hung.

Fairford Park is the site for the steam fair, usually in August. All through July, twenty miles round, you will meet the stately machines and their mahouts rumbling along the approach roads, and what fun the Fairford weekend is! Another big local event is the Ploughing Society's annual match in October, when young men with horse-teams from all the east Cotswold area compete in glorious effort, mud and enjoyment. They lay hedges too. All this goes on at different farms from Fairford to Burford. During the last war, the USA had an Air Force base here, which has now been turned into a flying-ground for Concorde. Now, as the extraction of gravel south of Fairford moves on and the pits fill with water, a big recreation and naturalist's area is developing. The area between Fairford and Lechlade is roughly one half of the new Cotswold Water Park which has already 1,000 acres of water and is expected, together with the South Cerney-Ashton Keynes-Somerford Keynes area, to provide 4,000 acres of lakes by the late 1980s. Roads are already being built or linked to carry an increasing volume of recreation traffic.

From Fairford the road runs north for about twelve miles along the line of the Coln and the picturesque Coln villages. Eight of them lie along the stream, with no main road to bring good and bad influences: Quenington, Coln St Aldwyns, Bibury, Ablington, Winson, Coln Rogers, Coln St Dennis, Fossebridge – Hatherop and Calcot are just off the river line. Value does not lie in any one particular village, but in the succession of them along a continually changing stream, all set in green or wooded hills, with old stone bridges and beautiful simple houses. These small settlements show an early discipline to limitations, to hard work in the fields, the lambing-pens, sheep-washing, sheep-shearing, the quarries, stone masons' sheds, builders' sites. Through this discipline the people learnt a knowledge of material, a sensitivity of eye and hand, a grasp of opportunity and of restraint, which cannot be learnt any other way. Travel up the Coln valley roads with an open heart and eye, and you will have gained an investment which will never fall in the market.

Quenington first, a hill village climbing from treasured riverside houses and gardens on the banks of the Coln, steeply up the sheepwalk wolds. All the little stone houses are fitted into the rise. There is a post office and shop, the *Keeper's Arms* and the *Earl Grey*. An old hurdle-maker is still at work. In her porch a young woman was sitting doing embroidery on a frame.

A big arched gateway into Quenington Court is a fragment from a preceptory of the Knights Hospitallers in the thirteenth century. Godwin's pump factory has been here for ninety years, first making deep well-pumps and the iron-sailed wind-pumps one still sees on farmland. Now the firm makes modern pumps, but its big export field includes such iron wind-pumps and also village pumps, for developing countries.

On the road to Coln St Aldwyns we looked back to a most striking view of Quenington roofs and mill behind us. Then we dropped down into the valley of the Coln, suddenly wide and green like a setting for a masque or pageant, the silver river

40

washing level with the grass in its long curves. The mill juts up suddenly, screening the village street. Pause to stand on the road bridge there, and you can hear a sighing moan from the millrace and stream coursing under the road, rushing out round a daffodil-planted island to rejoin the river in the meadow.

Round the sharp corner made by the mill, the plain, beautiful street rises up. These are cottages built with an eye to such harmonies as a continuous level of front garden walls, a continuing pattern of street doors set well in to give a moment's approach to the houses and a line of recurrent shadow, a meaning underlying the outward form, no doubt unconscious but in the eye and instinct for proportion and form. Here is the *New Inn*, log fire, good food, where we stayed. The village street leads up to the old church and kindred buildings of manor house, village school, shop and post office, from which little lanes creep out.

Before going on up the Coln to Bibury, we turned off on the road east to see Williamstrip Park, Hatherop and Hatherop Castle. Williamstrip Park is the home of Lord St Aldwyn, breeder of pedigree sheep, countryman and farmer 'as farming should be did'. We went into Hatherop Castle (which in term-time is a girl's school) to see the annual exhibition of the large group of Cotswold painters and sculptors called the Fosseway Artists. Another joy of our detour was to see a second lambing-pen, completed by a shepherd's caravan with little stove chimney. As we stood and looked and listened to newborn cries and mums' re-assurances, we heard the low sky vibration of Concorde taking off from Fairford – and there she was above us, long bird-neck and beak, delta wing, all brilliant line and power.

Back to Coln St Aldwyns, up the main street, and into Bibury. This little place is ringed by the Coln running at the base of a curve of high, wooded hills. You drop down into Bibury at one end and climb out of it at the other. The grouping of the houses clustered under the hill and strung along the river field is part of Bibury's beauty. On the steep curve down, you catch a glimpse of the roof of the great house, now Bibury

41

Court Hotel, built in 1633; then turn sharp left into the group of cottages called The Square. You will have seen a lot of old stone cottages by this time, and much like each other. But now and then you may catch a sight of some different quality. This limestone, firm but not hard, can draw the mason on, and when he is just the right man, rightly learned, he can draw response from the stone. He does his daily work with its usual problems, and on some days a living quality emerges, not expected in stone, a subtlety, a tenderness, a warm creative participation. It cannot be copied, but you can recognise it – in this corner, not in that, in Little Barrington church roof, in a dovecote here or there, in this whole cottage, not in that. Walk about Bibury and look at the roofs, the dormer windows, at the tiling of the gables and the 'valleys' between gable angles. The stone itself is local: it probably came from the big stone-mine at Quarryhill, a mile to the west of the village.

Bibury church keeps a considerable part of its Anglo-Saxon origin, and also rare Scandinavian ornament on the outside wall from pre-Norman times. The churchyard is full of table-tombs, headstones, ornamented by travelling carvers such as Jude Fawley, and country names. The river bounds it and the woods rise up steep and sheltering to the east, so that the place is chill in the early mornings and warm and long-lighted in the evenings.

Out of the square, the village street runs beside a stretch of the Coln in a flood field inhabited by ducks, with the well-known cottages of Arlington Row at one end, and at the other an arched bridge, Arlington mill, and the *Swan* inn. Here the cars and crowds gather in August, and are catered for. But at other times the place gets on with its own life. The low wall along the river invites lingering, and the shallow clear brown water is promising with trout, raised in five acres of Bibury Trout Farm behind Arlington mill. You can cross a foot-bridge and walk up to Arlington Row and then along a cool path edged with marsh marigolds on the far side of the flood field to the mill. Arlington mill, with its cottage, is open to the public. It has the mill machinery, which works, a mixed museum of country crafts and small machinery, and some magnificent furniture

42

made by the Sapperton craftsmen Gimson, Waals and Sidney Barnsley.

On now between hedges of blackthorn snow to Ablington, village of barns immense even on the Cotswolds, one dated 1727, and the old, apricot-coloured Manor House where Arthur Gibbs lived. We crossed the Coln here, at a lovely point of the river, by millstream, island, willows, bushes and gardens, and went on for a mile and a half towards Winson. The road is solitary, climbing gently, cowslips delicately yellow in the fields. A van passed, with 'Winson's Red Poll Herefords Henriques' on it. Winson Mill Farm was the home of the author Robert Henriques who died recently, a man of this countryside, farmer, JP. Someone in Winson breeds peacocks; we saw them by the river road. One bird was standing on a ground-floor window-sill like any three-foot brown and green robin, and several were strolling in an enclosure with daffodils, cocks and hens.

Coln Rogers is neat and tidy like a chapter-end drawing in an old novel. How ancient the cottages must be, with stone mullions to the windows, and how comfortable they look, with their handsome chimneys, TV aerials, yellow sheets on the line, flowers and vegetables, and the iron plates in the road that show the presence of public services. Across the river is a high wall of wooded wold, at the base of which stands a seventeenth-century rambling house, and a big garden running up the wold side. The church is a special Cotswold treasure, having a high Saxon nave and chancel which have survived almost as they were built, plain stone, archaic. An extraordinary central peace fills this small place. Outside, a recent tombstone, carved with axe and bull, commemorates a 'Byzantine scholar and much loved countryman'. Over the wall, rough-coated cows and calves moved quietly. Fools' parsley was breaking into foam under the bronze-leaved prunus. St George's flag flew on the little tower, a rare welcome sight to an English eye.

Calcot's single street lies on a steep, bare wold across the river, open to wind and larks. A buzzard watched us from a telegraph-pole. There were notices of the Coln Valley cricket team and the Coln Valley Village Hall. In *A Cotswold Village*

43

Arthur Gibbs relates a wonderful drama of the Coln Valley cricket team of which he was a member, and of a match which belongs to all happy English annals.

Coln St Dennis comes next, a more groomed village than the others, with specially fine gardens large and small, and specially cared-for houses large and small, and a Norman church definitely small. The valley is wider here, river on one side of rough, wild ground. Every yard of this water and its banks is treasured. Hedges were a drift of blackthorn blowing on the wind. In April, gardens along the Coln valley are opened and the visitor can walk along a millstream bank under the willows of an old mill-race island thick in silver and gold of narcissus and daffodils.

On the last bit of road up to the Foss Way, we turned to look back on the green land, rich roofs and strict grey walls, the silver stream glinting in and out of delicate blossoming spring copses. As we climbed, the valley moved away, becoming again a world of imagination, not of dream for it was real, but beautiful, lasting and potent. Soon we could hear traffic again. Below the road, Fossebridge millhouse roofs showed for a moment, and we came out onto the Foss Way. As we looked back from there, the Coln valley had disappeared, was only a fold in the wolds.

By the river crossing, the *Fossebridge Hotel* has made shady walks along the river and millstream and, when we were there, these were blue with forget-me-nots.

Turning towards Cirencester, we were soon at 600ft, with the wolds spreading all round us, on the road built by the Romans in huge, continuing swoops. The formation of the old Midland & South Western Junction Railway from Cheltenham to Andover comes in to the tiny former station at Foss Cross, behind the *Hare and Hounds*. The station is now a timber yard. I used to go to and from boarding-school on this line, and later, in 1944, made a wartime journey home from abroad that brought me to Liverpool, to Cheltenham, and so to this little railway and the stations I knew by heart. In the *Hare and Hounds* a winter photograph shows a snow-plough clearing a track outside the pub through banks of snow. We had coffee and sandwiches here, and admired the county tug-of-war champions photographed with the landlord.

A lane from Foss Cross took us across country only occupied by hares and birds and moving air, to Calmsden, between low walls and fields of crops. Here we could see and feel the land itself, the lift and slope, the smooth rise which makes no sharp impressions and yet compels the eye and, like its stone, shows at vast moments of silent looking an intimation of love and response.

Calmsden is a tiny neat spot laid on lonely open country at the crossing of little lanes. Think of that picture of the snow-plough at work! The village has some early nineteenth-century estate cottages with a pretty glazing of diamond or hexagonal panes.

We cut back to the Foss Way and turned towards Cirencester. Off the road, on inaccessible wold sides trodden only by sheep, the pasque anemone still blooms, imperial purple flower and feathery leaf. After half a mile we picked up the Welsh Way going off left to Barnsley and Ampney Crucis. The Welsh Way is the route-name given to those old roads hereabouts along which, before the days of railways or lorries, cattle were taken to Smithfield after fattening on Welsh pastures. The drovers of these big herds kept to ways far from traffic and toll-gates, where there was good grazing on verges by the road. This particular stretch of country down to Barnsley is varied and broken, with ragged remains of quarries – in fact, a grand area for sport. Sheep and lambs were feeding in long grass, a new sight to me, and the hedges were twinkling with chaffinches.

Barnsley is a well-cared-for village, but horribly split by traffic on the A433. The vicar here used to let his glebe fields to the drovers for the night. David Verey, the architectural chronicler of the Cotswolds and all Gloucestershire, lives in Barnsley. The village has a terrace built in 1851, just before the agricultural depression took hold. The date 1698 is cut on the cottage at the turn down to the church. In the church I found the window under the tower particularly absorbing in its strange representations of the burning bush, of the Red Sea being turned back (just like a mattress), and of Moses' rod and snakes, and other

45

subjects guaranteed to take your attention off the sermon.

Keeping to the lanes, we cut straight south to Ampney Crucis, crossing Roman Akeman Street at the edge of a wood. No houses here, but big herds of Friesian cattle, and sheep and more sheep, and cloth of gold of dandelions. Early April is the wine-making season, and you must pick the dandelions in the cool of the morning when the milk-sap is up.

New building at Ampney Crucis is on the top of the wold, and old Ampney straggles down past the *Butcher's Arms* to the big house, the church, the mill and the cricket field. As children we used to bike to Ampney, then push the bikes uphill to the *Butcher's Arms* and drink ginger beer under the apple tree. The mill still has a waterwheel which occasionally drives a saw. A little bridge over the Ampney brook separates the village from the main road, and thick trees shelter the mill, its island and the little church. The letter-box here bears an Edward VII monogram.

The Ampney brook gives its name to three more small places. Along the main road you come to Ampney St Peter, with Ampney St Mary on a lane behind. The brook then turns south and threads through silent pastures to Down Ampney, and on to add its drop to the Thames below Cricklade. To follow it, we went by Harnhill and Driffield. A winding road, overgrown little quarries, patches of old cultivation become rough verges, and a myriad birds take you there. A mighty Cotswold stile, two steps up to one enormous slab, leads to Harnhill churchyard path. What violets we found there, what crisp lords and ladies! Driffield has a proper duckpond, with muddy surround and ducks, right in the middle of the village – I've never known it dry, even in the hottest weather.

From Driffield the country road winds to Ermin Way, the main road from the south through Cirencester to Gloucester, on which we turned left for Down Ampney. On the way we passed a new road into the other half of the Cotswold Water Park, which we shall visit later. Down Ampney is hidden in gentle stream country, lanes winding with the streams, peaceful farms in little dips screened by elms, but the church spire guided us from miles away. Wiltshire may intrude, but in a few turns a tiny stone bridge carried us over the County brook safely back into Gloucestershire. There were daffodils on the village green, herds of pedigree cattle in the fields, men repairing roofs and walls and building a few new bungalows. We went down the farm road to the church where Vaughan Williams' father was vicar when Ralph was born. The great house is from the fifteenth century, which is long-lasting indeed. The church has had some lively years recently. The neighbourhood gathered to celebrate the eight-hundredth year of its dedication, and in Vaughan Williams' centenary year we all gathered again for concerts and thanksgiving. I had time then to observe a window in the south transept, of water scenes and storms. The inscription says it was a thank-offering for the preservation of a whole ship's company from wreck during the gale in the Black Sea off Sebastopol in November 1854.

What joy there is in early spring in these quiet places! In the churchyard, silence held the cawing of rooks and the soft cooing of two pink-grey doves in a budding tree. Against the wall was a row of crown imperial fritillaries among primroses. Returning along the winding lane we passed a coal lorry delivering sacks, a country sight. The children were homing from school, trailing along the hedges or swinging all over the road on bikes. Ralph Vaughan Williams made a great tune to the hymn on love, 'Come down, O love divine,' and called it 'Down Ampney'.

To see something of the Cotswold Water Park and the gravel-bearing villages of this area, we cut straight across Ermin Way from the Down Ampney road into the turn marked Cerney Wick. The country is rather like that round Inglesham, as much water as land, small poor plots of pasture, unchanged through centuries, huge willow trees and thickets. Before the first cottages of Cerney Wick we crossed the Thames & Severn Canal, with a lock and round-house for the lengthsman. Five of these were built for canal staff who were each responsible for a length of canal. The Stroudwater-Thames & Severn Canal Trust plans to restore the canal, and so the through-water route from the Thames at Inglesham to the Severn. Immediately over the canal we crossed the river Churn, hastening fast and clear over its gravel bed to join the Thames at Cricklade. One can walk along Cerney Wick's street and see big mounds of soil heaped beside lakes, which spread south-west for five miles. Farmland and trees have gone, hedges, thickets, blackberries, crabapples, cowslips, rabbits have gone, walks and picnic places are vanished into the past. But don't most people prefer lakes, boating, swimming and fishing? Drowned footpaths, even a drowned village road are usually exchanged for others, thousands of trees are being planted, water-birds and plants are increasing, a hotel and a sports hall are planned in Cerney Wick. Few will regret the rough, small-scale water-meadow country of wild hedges which often made tunnels over muddy forgotten paths, the huge elms and silver-grey willows; the great stone stiles round which the cows pushed gaps; the stone-slab culverts over drainage ditches in the fields, the planks across the clear and gentle stream; the little pastures with sorrel and buttercup and cowslip; the ditch-banks of violets, nettles, briar roses, brambles, and the half-wild ponies snorting and starting in damp shade or snatching at spring grass.

The countryside has changed, and the villages will be affected. There are new housing and camping sites, and new recreational facilities. The Water Park Committee and the County Councils concerned have worked out plans which in-clude nature walks, nature reserves, foot- and bridle-paths, camping and picnic areas, and new lakeside building of a stan-dard appropriate to our Cotswold tradition. I am thankful. The land between lakes might all have been sold for building.

Cerney Wick has the last mill on the Churn, a big new sluice for controlling floods at this close point to the Thames, and a pub, the *Crown*. The wild, lonely, twisting lane on flood-ditches leads from it to Ashton Keynes, Somerford Keynes and Poole Keynes, all villages afloat in the Water Park. A thread of the Thames runs along the street in Ashton Keynes, bridged by each house and walled with aubretia, fern, gold-dust and white arabis. Ashton uses for fences those tall, thin slabs of stone, 2ft across and 3ft high, that come from certain quarries (one at South Cerney) and are a Cotswold feature, needing no maintenance and taking no goodness out of the garden soil. Old and up-to-date mix closely here. A dairy-farmer is partner in the Ashton Keynes firm which rebuilds vintage and classic cars, getting its custom from the Argentine, Japan, Germany, Iran. He has also established on his farm a 7-acre vineyard. Most villagers run down their own village, but no Ashton man does, and Ashton men or women living four or five miles away are in exile until they can get back. Ask them why, they can't answer, but they know, and they get back. Ashton has a little church tucked away on a road outside the village, with a pleasant footpath to it from the riverside street.

We made now for South Cerney, my own village, and also the other main Water Park village, across the new spine road which connects the Keynes Water Park lakes between the A419 and Oaksey. A pretty inn, the *Royal Oak*, is handy to the new recreation field. A very old cross with a modern ball atop stands on a daffodil-planted green at the T-turn to the old bridge, church, and centre of the village to the left. Bradley's have a building material factory here, and gravel-water spreads out behind it in blue lakes, grey willows and white sails. At dusk, hundreds of gulls gather and subside for the hours of darkness. Loyalists persist in hearing nightingales in the withies, and I am sure they do.

The gravel firms have been a big source of employment in recent years, and keep young people and money in the villages. In the building expansion after the war, Edwin H. Bradley & Sons Ltd of Swindon took a leading part in developing reconstituted stone made from crushed limestone aggregates and cement which could be laid by any builder, being in standard sizes and shapes. So housing estates on the Cotswolds are of stone colour, toning, some well, some badly, with the old cottages. But the crowning beauty of Cotswold houses has always been their stone slate roofs, and no artificial roofing material has ever come near to their colour or quality. Now Bradley's have produced roofing-slates which look like stone, as I saw at Bourton-on-the-Water. They are made at Ashton Keynes, and Richard Bradley the chairman and managing director took us over the plant.

Gravel crushing and screening is done at South Cerney, and here also various Bradstone products are made. Clay is washed away, the gravel goes for crushing and screening, then cement is mixed in. At Ashton Keynes the roofing-slates are formed in moulds of polysulphide rubber that have been taken from natural stone tiles to reproduce their thickness and rough surface. These are held in wooden frames for handling and moving along conveyors. The aggregate mixture is poured into the moulds, which are then stacked in their frames. Pigment is added, giving a varying effect much more like natural stone. Finally, they are cured. We nipped in the wind and rain round the wide, open yards and saw stacks of twenty-nine different sizes, four or five widths to each size, and also ridge-pieces – along with building-blocks, drip-stones and mullions, special headstones for individual orders, and big piles of aggregate.

The river Churn gives its name to both Cerneys, one north and this one south of Cirencester. There are two former mills at South Cerney and a delightful walk between the river and millstream called by the old folks 'Between Brooks' and now 'Bow-Wow', for no reason one can rely on. The old bridge crosses both, and with the pool beside it makes a centre among the prettiest houses of the village, handy to the *Eliot Arms* and the *Old George*. Two lanes go off by the bridge: School Lane past old cottages and the former school, the thatched village hall, the old forge and a cottage grouping round the stream, an old mill beyond; Church Lane, rather stern, but leading past two manor houses to the church and a footpath that leads back to Bow Wow at Lower Mill. Part of the track and station site of the Midland & South Western Junction Railway remain, and some curious brick multi-arched road bridges over it, thought to have been necessary because of the flood-prone nature of the land in the 1880s when the railway was built. One of these bridges, that on the direct Cerney Wick – South Cerney road, has been by-passed and kept as a viewpoint for the Water Park. The canal comes up from Cerney Wick past derelict locks, and crosses the fields to go under the Cirencester road on its way to Sapperton. The wharf cottage remains, and the old towpath, restored by the village trust, is one of the best wild footpaths in

Lechlade mill. This charming house has a stone-tiled roof and porch, and stone lintels and sills to the windows. The miller chose a cut-stone arch and keystone for his stream, and a stone seat over it

Cirencester. The church tower makes the beauty of the Market Place. Showing here are the lines of the south aisle and pinnacled Tudor nave. In front is a three-storey building of 1490, now the church porch. Beside it the exteriors of two old houses have been altered and their upper storeys 'raised' behind parapets in eighteenth-century fashion. The market is in progress

the parish. No further indulgence about my village. But you will appreciate the church, and its special treasure displayed in a niche under the tower.

We left South Cerney for Cirencester by Silver Street, past the twelve clergy almshouses of Edwards College and the village's oldest farmhouse. Scores of peewits were crying keenly as they wheeled in their rising and dropping flight, or walked, crested and green-shining, on the ploughland. We passed the former aerodrome, and then a crenellated tower which was once a windmill base, and later a house. The river Churn rejoined our road after a big turn through the fields from South Cerney. We crossed it on turning left into Ermin Way for Cirencester, beaconed by its church's sky-drawn tower.

The tour described in this chapter falls within OS 1:50,000 map No 163 (Cheltenham and Cirencester)

Cirencester to Northleach

All roads lead to Cirencester, the church tower drawing the traveller down them to itself. The market place and the church are indeed the heart of the town, which stands on the site of the Roman Corinium but shows the grace and style of English country building in the seventeenth, eighteenth and nineteenth centuries, and much good work of the twentieth. David Verey says that the small streets immediately behind the church contain 'more genuine survival here than in any other town in the Cotswolds'. Gosditch, Dollar Street, Gloucester Street, Thomas, Coxwell, Blackjack, Silver and Park Streets and Cecily Hill, show Cotswold building in all its styles and purposes. Thomas Street still has little fifteenth-century Weavers' Hall almshouses, managed by the Weavers' Guild, and a seventeenth-century Friends' Meeting House; weavers' cottages face cloth merchants' houses in well-known Coxwell Street; Lloyd's Bank in Silver Street occupies one of the most beautiful houses in the town – but visit it and see.

The church is the biggest, and also the finest, parish church on the Cotswolds, its three-storeyed porch the largest church porch in England. In fact it was built for the business work of the medieval abbey, and only formally became part of the church in the eighteenth century. The upper rooms continued to serve as Cirencester's town hall until the urban district council (set up in 1894) provided its own offices. The roof of the entrance is sturdily fan vaulted.

Inside, when I step down the worn stones into the high, dim, spacious nave, I find refreshment for spirit, nerves and soul, or, one could say, priest, doctor and friend. Immensely tall, slim-shafted pillars carry the dark roof at a breath-taking height. A line of clerestory windows includes the seven-light window over the chancel arch. The great east end glows softly with delicate medieval and later glass. Round it cluster chapels rich in carving and history told in tombs and brasses. A particular treasure is the pulpit, wine-glass shaped in stone, one of the few such survivals in Gloucestershire from before the sixteenth century.

On the west side, the church is well set in new stone-paved surrounds. The great south porch and the nave form part of the Market Place, while the east end is screened by houses. The Market Place is wide, for once lines of buildings ran down the middle. Its big houses are much older than they look, for most of them have been given eighteenth- or nineteenth-century fronts, painted in soft, well chosen colours, and shops at ground level. Search out the churchyard, and see them from behind. The Forum, a big new layout of car park, open space and ways through to other streets leading off the lower Market Place, is sited close to the Roman forum. The rest of the town lies fairly compactly round this centre, with some big new housing estates further out. The large modern school is outside the town in the Deer Park. Behind the church are the Abbey Grounds, a beautiful leisure space close to the streets, owned by the town. This is the site of the medieval abbey, and later of a private estate that was planted with trees and shrubs of rare or special interest. The Churn, otherwise hardly enjoyed in the town, flows through them.

Lord Bathurst's Elizabethan house, The Mansion, or Cirencester Park, is in Park Lane, behind the big hedge. Cecily Hill, a broad rise of graceful houses (including a Tontine building) leads up beside it to the gates of his park. This was laid out in the great age of English landscaping from 1714 onwards, when the then Lord Bathurst planted yew trees round the forecourt of his house and designed the park to open out behind it. The yew hedge is now about 37ft high, highest yew hedge in the world. In designing the park, Lord Bathurst worked with the poet Alexander Pope, known for his eye for country. A superb central ride runs from the gates on Cecily Hill; others leave it at intervals, and run all the way across country to Sapperton. At the end of many of them lies, small and distant, Cirencester church tower. Now, farming and forestry take up much of the land; farm 'look-ins' are organised in season. The rest is open to the public for recreation of all kinds, but cars are not allowed. A leisure centre is being developed.

Old footpaths and walks lead through miles of beech woods and open land. As a local child, bluebells in spring and nuts in autumn took us to the Park for family picnics every year. A polo ground is here and a junior club ground with play, open to the public, every Sunday in the season. Horse and pony trials and competitions are also held here, often joined by younger members of the royal family and keenly followed by the public. Cricket, nature trailing, balloon ascents, police dog or sheep-dog trials, the driving of harness horse and pony turnouts, every outdoor affair in which Cirencester is interested goes on in the Park.

Cirencester is keenly aware of its Roman predecessor Corinium, even more so since the opening of its new Corinium Museum, which is a surprising pleasure to find. A Roman family talking in their house, a man working on fragments for a new mosaic decoration, the hooded gods of the locality, a shepherd's cote, faces from the medieval abbey, familiar things and tools from life, work and transport to the day before yesterday meet you as you walk through. The mosaic of the little hare, recently found in Cirencester, has become the symbol of the museum. Here too is the less conspicuous but world-famous Paternoster acrostic.

Cirencester is the centre of the south-east Cotswolds. The big sheep fair in September, two medieval Mop hiring fairs in October, a Christmas sheep and cattle fair, and a race meeting just outside the town at Siddington in March mark the rural year. The Royal Agricultural College brings keen specialists and students to the area. Good music abounds, from the church choir, choral society, keen school staff and town groups, for the Three Choirs Festival of Gloucester, Worcester and Hereford has spread its influence for music deep into its area over two hundred years. Industry and business, too, are active, much of it on the well-placed industrial site close in but not visible to the main town. And the shops! Cirencester has all kinds, but includes high quality small ones run by owner and family, some of several generations. These are mostly, not all, in the Market Place or adjoining it: Hayes the saddler and leather-worker, for instance, is a member of the Guild of Gloucestershire Craftsmen.

Friday is market day (there is a smaller one on Monday), and then you see the town as the centre of its countryside. What home-made dishes, cakes, jams, pickles, what estate-raised vegetables and plants, what fripperies and bargains from midland factories on the stalls in the Market Place! The town shops too are packed, offering Wye or Severn salmon, Coln trout, pheasants from big estates, turkeys, wood pigeons, eggs and fruit from local farms, many kinds of bread, and lardy cakes from village bakers. Everyone meets on market day, and the housewife leaves her bursting bags in the church porch while she has a good chat. Over all rises the tower, so tall that it needed two spur buttresses, which marked its delicate character for ever. The clock strikes the quarters and the hours, and at each third hour a tune is shaken out. You can climb this tower, passing the ringing chamber and the belfry with its twelve bells cast by Rudhall of Gloucester, the oldest ring of twelve in the country, and get the finest view that can be seen of the town, the beautiful mansion and spreading Cirencester Park, the Abbey Grounds, and the countryside all round.

Cirencester keeps a proper quality, a perspective of long history which checks vulgarity, a sense that you can live as you would like here, that values still hold. Quiet groups of modern houses or flats are tucked away out of the bustle yet not out of the life. Crowds disappear with the country buses and cars, and the grey-gold streets show their shapes again.

The town stands on a cross of the Foss Way and Ermin Way. These two contain the high wolds of the central Cotswolds, with the Churn valley and the Cheltenham road up the middle and the Salt Way or White Way climbing straight over the top to Winchcombe. It is all farming, riding and sporting country such as the Cotswolds have been through many centuries. Some is thickly wooded, most is rolling pasture or farmland, where water is precious and the light soil bears delicate-coloured lime-loving plants, cowslips, cuckoo flowers, lady's bedstraw,

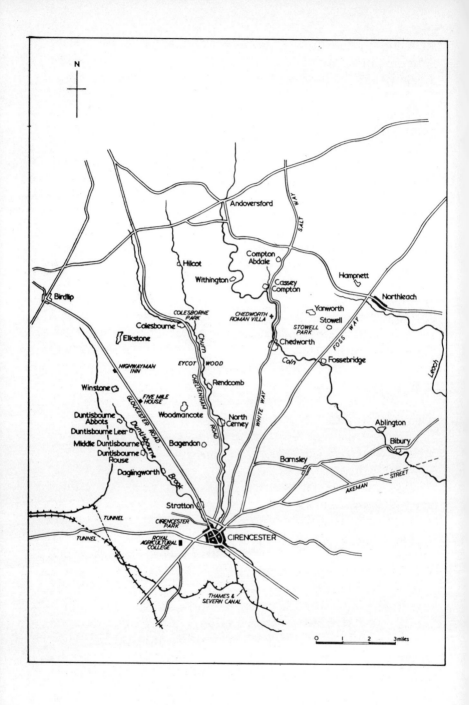

N

Andoversford

SALT WAY

Hilcot

Compton
Abdale

Withington

Cassey
Compton

Hampnett

Birdlip

Northleach

COLESBORNE
PARK

CHEDWORTH
ROMAN VILLA

Yanworth

Stowell

Colesbourne

STOWELL
PARK

Elkstone

Chedworth

Churn

HIGHWAYMAN
INN

EYCOT WOOD

Caln

FOSS WAY

Fossebridge

Winstone

FIVE MILE
HOUSE

CHELTENHAM ROAD

Rendcomb

Leach

WHITE WAY

GLOUCESTER ROAD

Woodmancote

Duntisbourne
Abbots

North
Cerney

Ablington

Duntisbourne Leer

Bagendon

Bibury

Middle Duntisbourne

Duntisbourne
Rouse

Duntisbourne Brook

Daglingworth

Barnsley

AKEMAN

STREET

Stratton

TUNNEL

CIRENCESTER
PARK

ROYAL
AGRICULTURAL
COLLEGE

CIRENCESTER

TUNNEL

THAMES &
SEVERN CANAL

0   1   2   3 miles

angelica and myriads of tiny beauties hardly showing above the soil or out of the old stone walls. Many shrubs mix with the glorious may – wayfaring tree, guelder rose, spindle, elder, briar rose, varieties of willow, crab apple. Travel slowly, and you will be rewarded all the way.

At the northern edge of Cirencester, Ermin Way (locally, the Gloucester Road) runs dead straight for twelve miles to the escarpment above Gloucester. Half a mile out of the town the road towards Cheltenham forks to the right. A mile along the Gloucester road a turn left leads along the valley of a small brook, the Duntisbourne, to five little places of great beauty in a rough country setting, Daglingworth and the four Duntisbournes. In Daglingworth the little Duntisbourne runs under a succession of stone arched footbridges in field and cottage garden-path. The village rises up the wold from the stream, with easy, beautiful house and cottage groups. Worn steps for drawing water from the stream remain, perhaps as old as the medieval dovecote which can be seen from the road. Nowhere is there better setting of cottages into the lie of the land, and I was happy to find a new group set with just as keen an eye.

Duntisbourne Rouse, Middle Duntisbourne, Duntisbourne Leer and Duntisbourne Abbots follow up the valley road. They are very small, immensely picturesque places, yet close to the big road and Cirencester schools and shops. Groups of young cattle wandered down to the fords, backing away from strangers, bluebells were part of the cottage gardens, tulips and irises of all the village scenes. Sheep and lambs, the same colour as the creamy stone walls, moved on the high sloping fields and a mighty ram stared haughtily from a shed doorway. What building! Haste had meant nothing in putting up these lintels, gateposts, stone water-troughs and channels through banks and hedges, these shapely cottages in a rough angle of land or above a spring, those steep gables and finials, the chimneys set into fitting stones. Need this skill and feeling be forgotten, even though we may change our materials?

There are two churches, at Duntisbourne Rouse and Duntisbourne Abbots, both perched between earth and sky. Saxon bright lads at Duntisbourne Rouse saw that if they planned the church on their really steep slope they would get a crypt or storage place holding up the farther end with very little digging. So we walked into the west end on the level and at the little altar we were off the ground, over a crypt. This tiny church, built with huge stones and Saxon herring-bone pattern in the walls, shoulder-width dark spiral stair with slits on to the brilliant buttercup fields, its saddleback tower, vaulted stone crypt and country carvings on misericord seats, has always seemed to me to be more than old and interesting, but wise, adult in love. The stone pillars and door-posts invite your hand to feel them. Here is communication, further than understanding. The church at Duntisbourne Abbots has a monument in verse to a servant of the Mesman family, which said, 'She lived not more to serve, than lived to love'. No servant of her own country and the City of God could achieve more, nor recognise it in another.

Out of this unnoticed valley we came on to the Gloucester road. Here the inn called *Five Mile House* is one you will not see the like of again. There are two little bars, each with a wooden settle and stone flags, a fireplace and a mantel with niches for mugs. The landlord is a friendly, sensible woman who has seen the world go by on the big high road for over forty years and has formed her own conclusions. She has not let her pub become a road-house or a haunt for school pupils, but keeps it as the local for all the small villages round, and for those passing who appreciate it.

We went south on Ermin Way for a mile and a half, then forked left to the Welsh Way through wild country to little Bagendon hidden in the wolds. Bagendon, older than Corinium, was the capital of the local area occupied by the Dobunni before and in Roman times. I feel sure that the country looks much the same as it did to the Dobunni. It may be less wooded now, though still patched with trees and bushes, poor humpy land, grazing cattle now much bigger, high wolds rising round the village and commanding the track along the Churn. There is a beautiful little church, memorable great barns and farmhouses and pretty stone cottages, all at different levels on an uneven woldside.

The Cheltenham road follows the wide pastoral valley of the river Churn enclosed in high wolds, part grazing, part splendid woods. One of the prettiest main roads in the Cotswolds, it was built new as a turnpike for horse-drawn coaches and waggons, and is skilfully graded. This Churn valley divides the heights of Ermin Way in the west from those of the Foss Way in the east. The little Churn winds gently through green pastures, its low banks bright with golden kingcups. Groups of delicate alders shade the occasional angler, footplanks link the valley where cows graze, while the wolds above are scattered with sheep. In early summer you can hear the baaing echo sweetly from all parts of the air.

North Cerney on this road is a mile from Bagendon. The new turnpike road cut the village from the church, vicarage and big house, and now the traffic is heavy. But the Churn runs along the road protecting the village side, with a bridge over to the pretty group of the *Bathurst Arms*, the mill and cottages, the manor house and great farm entry, and the steep street with post office, shop and small school, climbing up the side of the wolds to the White Way. North Cerney Farm breeds the black-nose and -ear Kerry sheep which you see on these wolds, and often wins the Kerry Large Flock competitions. Up the village street two springs are enclosed in rustic grottoes. There is new building, and the sound of a little works in an old barn. Spring gardens crowd every yard, lilac, broad beans, pea-sticks and raspberry canes.

North Cerney has a particular treasure in its church, across the road. This is one of the widely known Cotswold beauties. The exterior looks little more than any village church, and did not prepare us for the delicacy and brilliance which awaited us inside. The stone of arch, pillar or pulpit is pale, the wood of roof and pews is light; these, with the bright gilding, the heraldic reds and blues, the organ case decoration, the clear brass of lectern and chandelier, the colour patches of stained glass, held us, and silenced quick comment. What can anyone pick out to mention? The pulpit cut out of one block of stone without a joint? The figure of Christ on the rood loft? Every detail is valuable to an eye that can absorb it, though our

61

modern eyes are accustomed to different forms. Here is something totally rapt in another life, and even a passing visit will carry away some glimpse of this particular country pattern of glory.

Further along the valley road is Rendcomb, across the Churn. The big house clearly seen on the slope is now Rendcomb College. This very fine house was built on an old site in 1863, by the architect Philip Hardwick. The magnificent stable block, up the village road, is now the school science department. The village is a lonesome one, but in itself it has character and charm from its buildings and airy siting. Hardwick also built cottages here: they pick themselves out as professionally designed. The church was built by Sir Edmund Tame the son of John who built Fairford church, and there are many resemblances. Rendcomb church door is the original one, with old ironwork and a lock-plate that has arabic numerals thought to be 1517. I like to look at the sycamore roof of the chancel and think that Stephen Price cut the timber from trees grown in the parish, and made it all in 1897, and is buried close by in the churchyard.

On the map, a tiny place like Elkstone appears conspicuous, in a big expanse of farming and grazing land crossed by few lanes. To get up into this pure country, it is best to take the turning off the Cheltenham road not opposite, but a few hundred yards north of the turn to Rendcomb, and climb slowly through the lanes. Some are metalled, some white, some have grass between the wheel tracks. Eycot, Woodmancote, Elkstone are names to draw the wanderer. Soon after you take this turning you see on the left Eycot House, a comfortable house backed into sheltering trees, with cream walls, dark stone roofs and crisp chimneys. While I was enjoying it I discovered that it was built in 1930 by Norman Jewson, fellow of the Cotswold craftsmen Ernest Gimson and the two Barnsleys. Why did this surprise me, and stir feelings and questions which 300-year old houses had not stirred? A living past? Can these dry stones live? Had I thought of them only as museum pieces, priceless, irreplaceable, threatened by every development of life? In a moment I was up to my neck in wonderings on the value of a past, of a good tradition, of priorities in work, in money-spending, in the daily sights around one. I made no attempt to answer these on the spot. The more I saw of the modern Cotswolds the clearer an answer might become.

At nearby Aycote Farm is a strange tower close to the farm buildings. The farmer thought it was a grass silo built 150 years ago, but a wise man, the curator of Stroud museum, suggests it was a windmill, used as a source of power to thresh and grind corn, cut chaff, chop mangolds, break cake, saw wood or turn a grindstone – 1820-40 was a go-ahead period on the land.

Past Eycot the lanes lead up through woods, fir plantations and sandy patches, out on to high open tops. We saw the masts of Winstone radio station and came out on Ermin Way. Here is a shivering, unhuman world with a far-away cold sky. Big flocks of sheep and patches of wild plum blossom caught our eye, as did the *Highwayman* inn. It is a nice pub, though we older ones can never accept the name instead of the original *Mason's Arms*.

We turned back off Ermin Way at 800ft, opposite the *Highwayman*, and made for Elkstone, at the head of a steep drop down the country we had just climbed by lane, to the Churn valley. Woods lie on both sides of Elkstone but the village is in the open. It is not a beauty, though a good deal of new building going on shows that people like to live there. Elkstone's particular treasure is its church, said to be the most interesting and best preserved Norman church on the Cotswolds. The quite magnificent doorway shows fierce fantastic heads and figures, over which Christ sits in majesty as over our frightful deeds and longings. Step into the tiny compact building, and see more dragons on the chancel arch, the penetration of the creatures into the very sanctuary roof. Here at that verge of triumph over the power of the holy they are clamped in a perpetual grip by the boss at the meeting of the rib-ways – and beyond them the tiny slip of an east window shines heavenly blue, and gold light comes through the yellow glass windows on each wall of the sanctuary: then you feel something of the strength that drove the Normans, the knowledge of terror and destruction within man which could

63

only be held down by power, by the conviction of God and of their own knowledge of Him. There is a priest's room in the tower, and a Mason & Hamlyn American organ from Boston, USA, in the nave. Outside, the churchyard gravestones look across wold tops to far wolds across the Churn.

Leave this silent, toilsome region and go north over well-named High Cross. Like many Cotswold crossroads there is no building here. The old coach road from Cheltenham comes up through Cowley, and from High Cross you can follow it at 800-900ft parallel to the Churn and the valley road. Here I saw hundreds of sheep, and clouds of crows. The baaing and cawing was lively and friendly. A hare, russet with black tips to his ears, was busy getting his dinner. Another crossroads shows the way down to the main Cheltenham road again, and Colesbourne.

Here the Churn passes under the road, coming from its source five miles off at Seven Springs, which we can best visit on another trip. Two miles up, at Cockleford, is the stream's most spectacular mill, down a steep drop from the road, and a small wood delightfully named Tomtit's Bottom.

Colesbourne church takes some finding, being deep in trees. When we were there, the roof was being re-tiled, and the whole building was swathed in dust and sheets. Tiles were stacked in the churchyard, in groups numbered 7, 20, 22, 8, 28 etc., according to the size of tile needed for the row on which the tiler was working.

H. J. Elwes lived at Colesbourne, at Colesborne Park (argue the spelling with the Ordnance Survey, please). He spent his life in botanical travels and study that made him famous, but for us he planted woods of unusual interest and beauty round his home. The Hilcot brook comes down through part of them, and forms a lake in Colesborne Park. We saw late kingcups round its dark-green water, and a pretty balustraded bridge.

Take the lane to Little Colesborne. A world of trees lies ahead, for Colesbourne woods climb the wolds and join up one way with Withington and Chedworth woods, and the other with Hilcot and Chatcombe woods almost to the top of Charlton Kings hill above Cheltenham, a wonderful seven or

64

eight miles. A world of woods, fine, well chosen and cared-for woods, full of birds, large striped snails and wild flowers and ferns which often live to your eye in carvings in old churches. You must greet the stripy snails with respect, for their ancestors came here in wicker baskets in Roman galleys and waggons as delicacies for the table, according to more than local lore.

As the road climbs out of the Churn valley, woods lie on one side, chirruping with birds, fields and open wolds on the other moving with sheep and lambs, wind-trembling early summer crops, pheasants pecking and screeching. May and late fruit blossom light up the hedges. The tractor coming down squeezes into a gateway on the narrow lane. Past the beauty of Staple Farm, on to the saddle between the Churn and Coln valleys, and we are up above the world on a trackway made after the enclosure movement had obliterated many paths by joining up scattered holdings of villages or man. Only the church tower and a roof or two show that Withington lies below us, concealed and dispersed.

The village, old and new, follows the semi-circular shape of the wolds round which the Coln runs, leaving a broad space of farmland in the middle. On one side of this space the formation of the Midland & South Western Junction Railway is a shelter for plants, butterflies and wild life.

How curious to come on a Cotswold village that is hardly to be found, deep in woods, high banks to its narrow lanes, twisting round one corner of antique stone-built cottages and old gardens after another! There are a number of big houses among the cottages, and the place looks prosperous. Part of the woods and the Coln stream have been made into pleasure grounds, particularly around the *Mill* inn and the neighbouring restaurant. Beeches and sycamores stand huge, and walnuts adorn many gardens. There is a Roman villa just south of the village. Experts think that, although it was burnt, the villa and estate did not fall into ruin like Chedworth, but that the incoming raiders saw its value and took it over, so that it had a continued existence from Roman days through the Dark Ages into the revival of common life and order in Anglo-Saxon England. It is certainly alive now. Farming and forestry are

65

prosperous, football, cricket and darts thrive in village life, and there is a vigorous flow of visitors.

A footpath beside the churchyard leads down a most delightful, shaggy, wild-flower way under a bridge of the old railway (showing in its arch where the structure was widened to carry the double track that never was built) and a kissing-gate into the farmland space across to the other end of the village. Standing in the deep cool shadow under the bridge I watched buttercups and swallows reflecting and flashing sunlight. The only sound was the whirring of tiny winged creatures in the fool's parsley crowding round the gate.

Climb out of Withington past the Mill House, straight up a country road between high green banks and white may to the blue sky, and come out suddenly on the top and see all the wolds spread round you decked, mile after mile, in creamy, glorious, light-holding, light-giving, queen-of-the-year may. Past the big wood of Compton Grove and all the way to Compton Abdale – where would you be given such splendour, such lavishness of brilliant beauty as this may? The roll of the land is huge, the holdings and farms in scale; all is expansive, magnificent in our cool Cotswold style.

Down, down, out of the wind, into folds of the land where young cattle are grazing, into Compton Abdale that lies on the old Salt Way. A spring pours out of a carved stone creature's mouth and runs in a clear gravel-bottomed brook alongside the village street. The houses are built on slopes, farm buildings and barns in with the cottages. I saw old roof-tiles stripped off and stacked, and new, artificial ones being put on. Were they selling the old ones? I bet yes. On a huge barn, an exterior wheel on the wall shows that at one time a traction engine drove machinery inside the barn. The village buildings are less rustic than Withington, show more development.

A steep bank, blue with forget-me-nots, and a path of violets and hart's tongue fern go up from the street to the church. The tower has splendid gargoyles and carvings including Jack blowing his horn for the sheep in the meadow and the cow in the corn. On a flat tomb we saw a pattern of nine holes which people say was used in an old game: I would think like noughts and crosses. As we came down, we heard the brook again beside the road and saw the wagtails in the garden opposite.

An almost unknown beauty is hidden close to Compton Abdale, a mile downhill on the river Coln, Cassey Compton or Compton Casey. A plan of the house and gardens in 1712 is in Atkyns' *Ancient and Present State of Glocestershire*. It is a wide, two storey, gentle spread of late seventeenth century, and some older, building, with the river curving round it, in the deep bowl of the hills. One wing has been demolished, but the west wing, the main block with its easy but stately approach, the stable block and outbuildings establish a still centre, a sense of a complete life. The deer-park, the farm and farmland, cottages, pools and weirs for fishing, yew-hedge sheltered bowling green, gardens for kitchen, walking, observation, and the wolds for raising sheep, horses, cattle and poultry made it a self-supporting community. Now it sleeps in a deep seclusion. The huge, untrained yews were full of crows, the only noise in the valley bowl. However, on the green by the farm-cottages were children's tricycles and washing-lines. Two farm carts, painted yellow and red, looked practical and handsome.

We now followed the river road by the Coln along the edge of Chedworth woods to the turning to the Roman villa, one of the most famous excavated Roman sites in England. (There is another Roman villa site marked on the map much closer to Chedworth, so follow the signposts carrying the National Trust sign). This is a delightful spot for visitors, on a slope surrounded by magnificent woods, with the ground plan of the villa laid out and easy to grasp. It was begun in the years A D 100-150, as a series of buildings on three sides of the sloping valley. A spring rises in the north-western corner, and there the Roman owner built a little cistern and spring-house for the protective nymph of the spring. The spring still rises and the water runs, though time like an ever-rolling stream bears all its sons away and new sons come and park their cars and walk round to look at the rooms and patterned floors and deep, stone baths, and the child's coffin brings close the grief of 1700 years ago.

The villa now belongs to the National Trust. It was one of

about twenty-two such sites in this area, where self-supporting agricultural life combined with the civilising order, peace and culture of Rome. They were linked in a general economic interdependence with the centres of Corinium (Cirencester) and Glevum (Gloucester). The local Dobunni people were domestic, hard-working, skilled men. When the Romans landed in Britain, the Dobunni sent envoys and agreed with them before the legions even crossed the Medway in Kent. I was amazed to learn that the villa had been occupied, the land cultivated, for more than 300 years into the late fourth century or even the fifth, when the legions were withdrawn to defend Rome. Then the man whom we call Arthur, Roman-trained, held back the invading attacks for forty years – one more generation, which may have been crucial to Britain and to the incoming raiders.

When I asked the staff in the museum where the stones came from for the modern outlining and protecting of the rooms, they replied, rather shocked, that they were all dug up from the Roman building. The same one-handed, self-sharpening shears were used there as all through the medieval sheep and woollen industry for centuries – and as I use in my garden-clipping today. Room 32 is the point at which the discovery of the whole site began in 1864, when a gamekeeper was digging for his lost ferret, who had delved underground and not returned with a rabbit. He was probably after the hare in the hand of Winter in room 5.

To get to Chedworth village from the villa is a journey. You should go back along the river road to its junction with the Compton Abdale road, and turn left. On the turn you get a proper sight of Cassey Compton house. Then start climbing above the villa into Withington woods, the lane sunk in banks high above your head. These Withington and Chedworth woods stretch for five miles of light-filtering beech and crisp oak, not oppressively dense or gloomy. In spring there are quantities of windflower anemones, and later bluebells to make the light half water. You can roam and wander, lie on your back and feel yourself floating in this green inhuman element, while a sunshaft on the green sycamore flowers or the

Cotswold products: *top* Huntsmans Quarry shows layers of stone lying in the land, but breaking up to mix with soil at the top, leaving only a thin layer of turf. Yet the may bushes take hold; *bottom* Old Cotswold ewe and lamb; this old breed, whose wool made many Cotswold fortunes, is happily being revived

Lower Harford on the Windrush near Naunton shows the richer country of a river line. The gate is made of horseshoes, and the iron letters of the name are surely hand-wrought. A beech tunnel arches the lane

gold laburnum sings how merrily now you live under the blossom that hangs on the bough.

As you go up the lane suddenly the green vanishes, and you find yourself in the air and pure light, on the remains of an old aerodrome, in the middle of miles on miles of high wolds deceptively level, shimmering gently in and out of each other, young barley and wheat pasture chequered with stone walls, sheep and cows, turnip and hay grass. A strongly cut stone stile on the roadside may catch your eye. Turn left and left again to come down into Chedworth village, queen of the upper Coln. It is in three characters: first the incomparable group in a bowl of hills which meets you on this road, second an up-and-down-under-trees group, and third a group along the high top that keeps a snow-plough on the road verge.

Chedworth church and manor house, the barns with buttresses and gothic windows, the lawn sloping down to a pond and the running stream, the little terrace of cottages, with the *Seven Tuns* under trees down the slope, make this a village group worth seeking through the wolds and woods. Time moves even here, as a few fortunate modern cottages show. In the church the date of 1485, when the roses of York and Lancaster came together in a battle and a wedding, is marked on the lower face of the stairs turret in arabic numerals (ie the numerals we use). David Verey points out 'the early 4, like an uncompleted 8'. Only Roman numerals like X, V, I, were used until about the fifteenth century, and our modern ones came in very slowly as business, or liking for modern ways, compelled them. Verey adds that the use of arabic numerals, as at Northleach, reminds us that the Cotswolds were an international centre for wool buyers, and in touch with their modern world.

I was once here at Easter when the church was brilliant with primroses and daffodils; from a bunch of budding twigs in the nave dangled half-eggshells, painted all colours. There are six bells, five cast in 1717 by the great master Rudhall of Gloucester. The War Memorial board lists not only the dead, but every person who served, which always seems right.

The manor, with house, barns, stables and cottages, lies

round a bowl of low grassy hills. A few years ago Chedworth village acted a pageant of *Piers Plowman* in this bowl. Production was good and the mass of village actors keen and audible, village-made costumes, pasteboard court rooms and hell-gate just right. An orange sunset spread slowly behind the hill-tops and reflected its colour over the arena. Evening stillness and perception rose within the whole scene. Reader, I wish you had been there.

Chedworth of the many levels showed us glimpses of itself as we walked: a stream runs along the lower village street; the Congregational chapel with a quaint old slate roof that dates from 1804; a post office and stores, and the school up on the top level. On the lowest level I watched a string of stocky, grubby ponies leading a string of earnest small girls to a low wall onto which the small girls climbed to get onto the stocky ponies. An old craft still lives at Chedworth, for in the list of the Guild of Gloucestershire Craftsmen I noticed the addresses of a pair of weavers here.

For Yanworth and Stowell and so to our day's end at Northleach, we climbed again, a high empty road, stone-walled, with long views, may and beech, a few late cowslips still lightening the verge, a big herd of buff-coloured cows. At one point we got a sight of Stowell Park, home of Lord Vestey, of corned beef and polo fame.

Yanworth barns are bigger and more majestic than other barns, especially the one by the church with a tiny lantern and O window. Someone planted evergreen holm-oaks here, which add a dignity and ceremonial touch to groups of cottages and farm-yards. The tiny, intricate pattern of their leaves combines with the sturdy stone lintels and long dark lines of roof-tiles to provoke some cypher in the mind. The church is a little stone-flagged place, clean as a new pin, with patterns made from bits of old medieval glass, and a crisp starched bonnet carved in stone on a woman's head on a low base of an arch.

Close to the turning to Stowell a tiny stream crosses fields under flat stone bridges, or through culverts. There was sunlight and a light rain blowing when we were there, and a Hereford herd all red and white, grazing, so that

72

Blown by all the winds that pass
And wet with all the showers,
She walks among the meadow grass
And eats the meadow flowers.

Approaching Stowell, we were now within a great agricultural estate, where the people, land, crops, animals, trees, walls, gates, hedges, are cared for and maintained as part of a plan that bridges the generations.

The road to the church took us close to the famous polo stabling, which was worth a detour just to see – so austere, so absolute. But I wanted to see the church, the tiny dark centre of mystery that I remember, the painting on the wall of the Heavenly Court above and ourselves below, finding the unpersuadable justice. The door was locked – and no notice told us where to find the key. Was this an omen? Only two churches in this central area of the Cotswolds were locked, and the cause (in such a private zone) was unlikely to be vandals. The omen was against the locker, not the knockers at the door.

So, rather cross, we left Stowell, crossed the Salt Way, and came into Hampnett where the Leach rises. The angle of the road has produced a terrace of cottages with circular flights of steps up to each door, six steps for the first, five for the next and so on. Sunny small-holdings are laid out on a slope, and there are one or two very big, old curious houses. One looked to me as if a man had lived there fifty years and been found ten years dead surrounded from attic to cellar by mildewed wool sacks. Big flocks of sheep and lambs were round the village. The church is coloured inside in soft-patterned maroon, and all the arches are painted in roses. I hope they will survive 400 years to show archaeologists what a sweet and gentle century the twentieth could be.

From Hampnett you run down into Northleach, an old stone town with too much traffic, to choose a lodging off the long main road and the noise-hammered market place.

The tour described in this chapter falls within OS 1:50,000 map No 163 (Cheltenham and Cirencester)

By Windrush, Eye and Dikler

Northleach, just east of the Foss Way, is a village built like a town; a small place that was once a busy centre for the home and export wool trade. It has one long, main street sloping up from the central market place, a great church, many houses showing old wool-working or warehousing ancestry, almshouses of 1616 and several old inns. Set in open country, it could be delightful, but the A40 between Cheltenham and Oxford runs along the main street and across part of the market place. Northleach looks a little as though it had its eyes and ears shut, not because it is asleep, but against the destructive noise of traffic. However, out of season or in the rain when the stone glows gold, there is great pleasure in looking at the little town: there will be more, when the by-pass scheduled to be begun in 1978 is finished.

The market area has the old lock-up and wool houses, all three to four hundred years old. Little alleys lead you to a delightful miniature square, with a half-timbered butcher's shop, others for pottery and antiques, and houses of many shapes and sizes. A walk up the long main street takes you past quiet houses built in the seventeenth century and gradually altered to suit other times, and bright-flowered cottage corners and yards. Here are the Dutton almshouses, most charmingly antique outside and modernised inside, with all the traditional features: steep gables, finials, stone tiles, mullioned windows, the drip-moulds over them continuous along the bottom storey. The central arched doorway carries Thomas Dutton's initials.

Northleach's greatest treasure is its church, one of the constellation of Cotswold wool churches. From whatever point you approach Northleach, the mighty tower holds your eye, strong, intense, no battlements or pinnacles to break the line, but a whole, concentrated, convinced power in stone. The great

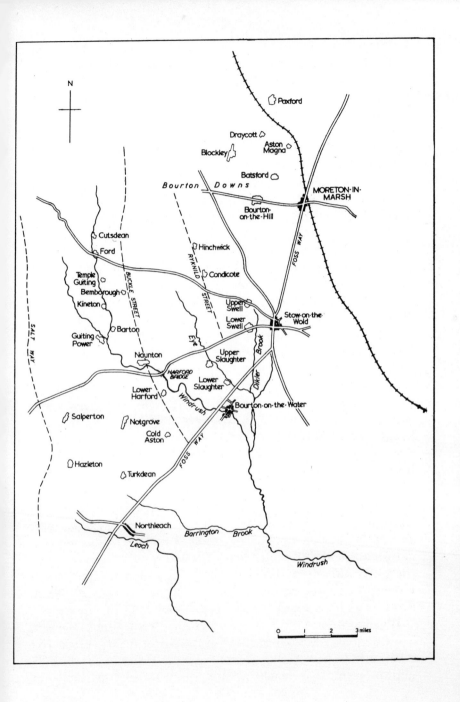

chambered porch has fan vaulting so fine that the stone ribs could be a handful of bamboo rods. Of particular interest are the masons' marks and the brasses. But the soaring, light-filled, delicate glory of the interior is an ageless, fresh discovery. The east window and much of the chancel and the seating are modern post-war Cotswold work of the best quality. Here is the past, the good tradition, the priority of values, alive and fructiferous among us for old and young.

Out of Northleach, at the Foss Way crossroads, is an unusual building, until recently the police station. It is the surviving portion of a country prison, built in 1789-91 to embody many reforms of those times.

Leave all behind and away into the wilds we'll go, to Turkdean, Hazleton, Salperton, Notgrove and Aston Blank. You can spell the second Haselton if you wish, and should call the last Cold Aston by resolution of the parish council, please remember, though the ordnance map is only half way to the change. June in the Cotswolds can bring a day grey-blue with heat, and long tree shadows across the road. The land is dressed with may, which in strong heat gleams as part of the light. Here is deep country, fool's parsley drowning verges and turnings; the inhabitants are chestnuts, beeches, elms, hawthorn, cows and calves, sheep and lambs. Water is precious. The landscape is bare with dry turf, except where a spring fosters groups of trees and plants which shelter birds and small creatures. Down through sun-flecked shade, buttercups brilliant against the green and cream, across a stream to Lower Turkdean. A few houses scatter along the valley bottom and up the steep hill on the other side to Upper Turkdean, the people busy in gardens and up ladders on stone-tiled roofs. This church claims foundation in the eighth century and to have been the first church in the Cotswolds. It contains a window of 1924 with a man in a modern suit, and on the porch-pillars are figures with headdresses carefully cut. Clothes mean something in Turkdean.

We came out on top of the wolds, barley trembling in the sun, a local quarry working, the may smelling heady. Have you noticed how barley shows more light and shade, more shine and smoothness, than wheat? Sheep press together in the shade.

The road dives 1 in 6 and up again, and there are pigs in the fields and under orchards, black and white, and ever-delightful pink. An old green road invites you to walk and lie in the hedge-shade. A Cotswold characteristic, a dry valley without stream or trees, shows the shape of the land in every small contour, undisguised by crops, structure like a creed. The road here is not even surfaced in the middle. Chequered brown butterflies are about. A van is collecting eggs from an island farm in the cream and green sea of the country.

At Hazleton, a rectangular little place of pale stone and light tiles and deep chestnuts in bloom in June, it struck me that a steady business was going on in stripping roofs and selling the stone tiles. Road walls too were in bad repair, and many out-buildings ruinous and stripped. The church, in its lovely set-ting, is pre-Norman. Marks in the porch are claimed to be votive crosses cut by pilgrims on setting out, not to Jerusalem as I expected, but to Hailes Abbey eight miles along the Salt Way near Winchcombe.

On the road up Pen Hill you get a view on your left of Cleeve Hill, highest point of the Cotswolds, looking rough and hazy on the horizon. Then a cool world of woods shades you, full of birds, while you see through green windows over bright open land.

If you go north through Salperton (where the old Bourton line reached the highest rail level in the Cotswolds) to the B4068 and turn right, you have a lonely run over wolds at 860ft carry-ing a wealth of sheep and glorious may. Will all us saints in heaven clad in robes of white and holding palm sprays look like the may clustered in thousands over the Cotswolds in June?

Two young ditchers were sharpening sickles on the second turn to Notgrove, which, on this B4068, I prefer to the first. A farm dog sitting beside the driver of a tractor panted a greeting. The village is on both sides of a steep, zigzag dip, and from this approach you can glimpse and enjoy the whole. Notgrove is the prettiest, happiest-to-the-eye village in the wilds. Stone-roofed cottages, porches and little decorations, gardens of mixed vegetables and flowers, the glorious spread of the manor com-plex of house, farm, buildings and stables which is my own choice of an ideal specimen of Cotswold building, the bronze-green walnut trees, splendid chestnuts, sycamores and copper beeches, swallows speeding from eave to eave, make this spot rich and beautiful.

The people here have a feeling of it. In the church is a needlework reredos representing the slope on which the village stands in the bloom of early June, with village, church and manor as centre of the panels. A border of hazel is for Notgrove's name. The work was done by women of the village – twenty panels in petit point and gros point. Eleven years went into the making, and in 1954 the great work was achieved and hung in the little sanctuary.

From Notgrove a straight lane leads to Cold Aston, farming wolds spreading for miles on each side, the air full of larks. A mighty wind-break or shooting-break of beech trees provides welcome shelter to animals and crops. The village, like an old picture, is partly under big trees and we found the sycamores all in bloom with long, light-green panicles. I noticed what good use some people made of yellow in their gardens against the buff stone, using irises and wall roses. A yard gatepost was cut from one enormous stone. The *Plough* inn is seventeenth century and little altered, except that it now incorporates the post office. In an outbuilding near it I saw old stone pillars, bigger than that gatepost. Cold Aston has a well-known stud, breeding golden, white-maned, white-tailed Palomino horses.

Back now past the Notgrove turn and on over the B4068 past Notgrove's long barrow – has it perhaps been a quarry for farm and village gateposts and cowshed pillars? On through Aylworth's farm, a medieval window reset in an eighteenth-century barn. Then over the A436 and down into the valley of the Windrush to run close alongside it to Barton, a beauty spot hidden under trees and high banks, with a farmhouse by the road that has a touch of medieval romance in its dignity. Kineton is a mile on, plain and simple, with a good Donnington pub called the *Half Way House*. The landlord lit a wood fire for us and the locals.

Lanes join Kineton to three old roads which run across the top of these central sheepwalk wolds: Salt Way on the west,

Buckle Street on the east, and our unnamed choice straight ahead, that climbs high up above the river line. Along this we came to Cutsdean, clinging to the 1,000ft rise of Cutsdean Hill. A mile north is Field Barn where the Windrush rises in a spring feeding a pool among alders and brambles. Miles of silent wold country lie round Cutsdean, one curve opening to another in changing depth in light and shade. Everywhere the subtle lines engage the huge sky. Cutsdean hamlet is a sturdy fortress of man in an unpeopled world of earth, grass, sheep and crops. The cottages are strongly built in stone with sheltering stone porches. A little semi-circular bulge shows the old boiler for washing day or Christmas puddings, neatly stone-tiled in six curved courses. Summer heat presses down on the slopes of thin soil, till you can smell the earth and tiny aromatic plants. In the long fading light of summer evenings, the little houses seem to lose substance, their lines and colour merging into the land and soft air.

We went back to take the B4077 across the Windrush through Ford, only a line of cottages along the road and a good pub, to work down the east bank into different country, one of gentle, river-watered land and villages. Soon we turned off the road, down into the ancient little Guitings (from the Old English 'gyte' meaning flood) a former name for the Windrush. How these Guitings have come up! In the long agricultural depression (1880-1930) before the last war they were sad, shabby, crumbling. Not so now, since money has poured into the countryside from subsidies, revived farming, new residents. Temple Guiting was once a possession of the Order of Knights Templar (hence Temple), and probably owes many qualities to this connection. The manor farm-house has the distinction of being considered the finest of small Cotswold Tudor houses. Of modern work, a new crescent built in dark timber, reconstituted stone and dark tiles is interesting.

Guiting Power is a little, grey-stone place, but unique in its movement for self-preservation. Its people experienced the usual danger of village houses being bought by strangers for weekend holiday cottages. Villagers formed a trust to buy cottages as they came up for sale, maintain them in character and modernise the interiors, and rent them at figures the village people could afford. This has succeeded, and the trust has been self-supporting since 1966. Good cottages stand round the green and square, with majestic trees setting off their simplicity. Two separate blocks of council houses are built of real stone, with traditional, big end gables. In the Norman church, the carved nave roof corbels include the heads of King Edward VII and Queen Alexandra. Well Lane offers a cool stroll past a very old bakery to a field gate and stile, and spring water. If you are here in late July you could go to the Guiting Music Festival.

A mile or so south-east of Temple Guiting is the new Cotswold Farm Park at Bemborough. In 1970, European Conservation Year, it was decided to start this park to conserve and help perpetuate all farm-breeds of these islands (including St Kilda, Man, and others offshore) and also breeds brought home from the crusades or later which have influenced our own. Post-and-rail enclosures have made good use of hollows, humps and bushes. Here are Old Gloucester cattle (which first produced Double Gloucester cheese), Chartley (pre-Roman) wild British cattle, the Old Cotswold breed of sheep, and Orkney sheep that only eat seaweed. Reindeer (the most ancient farm-animals in Britain), buff turkeys, old-time poultry of the most exquisite form and plumage are there. Bagot goats, ponies, Shire horses and farm-carts in which people can ride add to the fun. Some may gloat over the *Rocket* locomotive or the de Dion Bouton car, but I'm for the Old Gloucester cow, chocolate coat and white spine and tail, the Chartley bull, the Cotswold sheep, the Old Gloucester Spot pig.

We were there in early June, when the young families, including chicks and piglets, were highly mobile, especially six tiny ginger Tamworths, who had organised their own cross-country obstacle race. As I gazed upon the archaic form of the British Lop or English Landrace sow, warmly snoozing in a hollowed dell, and, having read that 'once a forgotten breed' she is now, with a change in market needs, 'staging a comeback', I exchanged with her a deep satisfaction.

80

From Bemborough Farm we turned right along Buckle Street, which here crosses one of the loneliest areas of the Cotswolds towards Naunton. On other journeys we have turned east at the first, unhoused, crossroads, along the contours to Chalk Hill and Swell Hill, a sacred way in old days, for tumuli and ten long barrows lie within two square miles of it, like the tombs along the Appian Way into Rome.

As I have stood above Swell Hill Farm at 740ft, I have felt a numinous influence, a sense of an area, however much used, sacred to a god. It was no longer lonely. The name 'swell' may come from 'swelgund' meaning a very deep place, a swallow-hole where stream sank into limestone – and we shall find this meaning when we come to Donnington millpond. Legend held that the god brings the water down into the earth to send it out in countless springs that feed pastures on otherwise barren heights. Our ancestors called a bleak stretch at Chalk Hill 'Cow Common' because the herdsmen found good grazing on the poor land. They built chambers for their dead in the keeping of the god, but knew the land was not theirs and made no settlement on it.

Over the crossroads we passed on our left the great Huntsmans building-stone quarry, to run over open wolds to a right turn and then a left. Naunton lies below in the valley of the Windrush, which has glided here through flowered meadows and woodland from Barton by Guiting Power. The village spreads on two levels, along the river line and behind on rising land, the church at the west end, the *Black Horse* at the east. I don't think I have ever seen a bigger beech than by Naunton church, which looks a little like a best Sunday stable with a tower. It has a beautiful pulpit carved 500 years ago.

There is some sensitive modern building on the steep land. Down by the river level a farm has its own ford, bridge and dovecote, with four little gables and a central turret, built about 1600. A mobile shop was getting a lot of custom as we passed it. Naunton expanded in the nineteenth century. Dale Terrace was built, simple working-class cottages, but still with a touch of dignity and a string course for decoration, and the school and Baptist chapel. An old man courteously showed me over this. A little room inside was the original chapel. Then congregations increased so much that in 1850 they built the big chapel you now see.

The road on from Naunton to Harford Bridge is a peaceful journey. The riverside banks are rich and sweet; freshness and colour move along with you. From Harford Bridge we strolled down a lane beside the Windrush to pretty Lower Harford and back again before leaving the river on the A436, climbing east across Buckle Street, then down and over the little Eye stream which creates Upper and Lower Slaughter. A field of potatoes made a deeper green. Half a mile brought us to where Ryknild Street (locally called Condicote Lane) crosses the road. This little known Roman road ran from the Foss Way near Bourton-on-the-Water to Watling Street near Wall, not far from Lichfield. We turned into it past huge windbreaks of beeches, and so came to Upper Slaughter.

These two villages, Upper and Lower Slaughter, bear a heavy burden of fame for their beauty and their siting on the river. They are all stone built, and nearly all stone tiled. The word 'sclotre' in Old English meant slough or muddy place. You must avoid the crowds' season and time of day. Then you can enjoy Upper Slaughter street with its stream down the middle, little stone bridges, the reflections, and the huge trees which give a scale and proportion to the cottage groups. Bigger houses are as good examples of Cotswold architecture for their style as the cottages are for theirs.

The top of the village slopes down to a ford in a green place where a long house with doveholes keeps gentle watch. Up the slope are the church and manor house, and a big Cotswold house that is now the *Lords of the Manor Hotel*. The gates of the hotel are on the village street, but the grounds wander away in privacy to fields and a lake. The manor house is behind the hotel, a grand Elizabethan (sixteenth-century) house built on earlier monastic foundations and remains, which has been restored and reopened.

Upper Slaughter church has an unusual feature, a chapel built in 1854 to house the tomb of the rector. It is a splendid work, with an old-style brass on the tomb and a richly carved recess which anyone might take as an antiquity. The old tradition was alive and at work. A memorial of 1910 to a gardener, a coachman and a servant is another affectionate tribute to employees, which gives good colour to the social relations of past time, so often ill-painted.

We met the Slaughter Herd of British Friesians on the lane to the church. There was no room for us among the broad black-and-white sides, shining black eyes, and ears each with a little clip. A man in a long coat down to his gumbooted ankles encouraged them with a twig switch, but they knew it was their road.

Lower Slaughter is equally enchanting. It is all close on the stream, with a green on one side round which the simple, beautifully proportioned cottages make the centre. Every detail gives pleasure. The shallow, clear brown water rustles over its stone and gravel bed under many footbridges. The old mill, built of brick, keeps its chimney and its wheel. A footpath walk is marked nearby. Here in winter, if you can catch the brilliant stillness of snow along stream edge and on gable angles as we did once, you have seen the best.

At Lower Slaughter do not overlook a row of Council houses in Church Furlong. This won the Festival of Britain award and carries the Festival badge on the end wall. They are houses of plain design, in natural Cotswold stone and roofed in Cotswold stone tiles. Big gables mark each end, and small ones each door. The row is simple, solid and something to be proud of, as good as any similar row built in old days.

It is strange to us now to think that these villages are the product of land workers', masons' and country craftsmens' life, skill, thoughts, traditions – worlds we can hardly understand at all. Yet they have a link with us if we will. When one looks at the layout, design and proportions of houses and streets such as here at Lower Slaughter, and the use made of the stream, one is aware of a sensitive seeing, an instinct for form, relationship and the worth of every piece of work, which passes into one with power to quicken the eye and strengthen the sensibility. To such villages now, the danger of disintegrating under alien building and living is always near. They are defended by planning committees and officials, their own councils and amenity societies, and the concern of people themselves.

As we took the country road to the Swells, we looked back at the lovely line of Lower Slaughter houses. Beside the lane, rooks walked in the young corn, and their black heads just above it shone in the sun. Young beef was grazing, beeches and oaks enriched the eye. Lower Swell, two miles from Lower Slaughter, is on the old Cotswold ridgeway, which was turn-piked and has become one of the roads into Stow-on-the-Wold a mile away. The compact village is all stone, with a war memorial, of urn and flame, by Sir Edwin Lutyens. The church is very old, but has good nineteenth-century wall paintings and glass. On the road out of Swell towards Stow, Spa Cottages and Spa House reflect a mineral spring discovery in 1807. The spa never developed and in time the spring ran dry. The little houses are decorated in a Hindu style, and are curious.

Below Upper Swell, a three-arched bridge crosses the Dikler. A mill with mill-wheel stands by it, and round its big pond old cottages are grouped. Young chestnut trees have been planted all the way up the hill to the rest of the village. The far end of the churchyard has a delicious view of the mill-pond below through yew trees. The *Golden Ball* in the village is a Don-nington house, and offers accommodation. Here are photographs of Swell United, winners of the local league. You can play darts, or quoits, or the piano. And you can hear a slow voice saying 'I thought 'eed say thaat'.

Half a mile north of Upper Swell is the Donnington brewery and lake, a great Cotswold treasure. To reach it from Upper Swell we turned west along the B4077, and then first right. We moved high above the Dikler valley, in a fold hidden from the road. The brook crosses beneath, a deep drop suddenly opened on our left, and there was the lake, and the handsome L-shaped brewery with one swan-and-cygnets weather-vane and one beer-barrel vane, two huge beeches, a croquet lawn, garden, and a series of huts and shelters for thirty varieties of birds.

The owner took me round out of sheer good nature, for of course he was busy – when not brewing he is answering en-quiries, or looking after peacocks, or black swans, or

84

persuading the blind white duck to feed. The beer is made from barley grown in nearby fields malted in Cirencester, Worcestershire hops and fresh spring water, raised to the top of the building by a great waterwheel made in Tewkesbury two hundred years ago. Up the ladder stairs we saw big wooden vats lined with copper, and biscuit-coloured froth on the gently fermenting beer. Ten employees and seventeen public houses, what a lovely little business in a Cotswold beauty spot! The lake is the old millpond, fed by the first springs of the Dikler from underground, north of Condicote over two miles away. A mill has been recorded here since 1327. In 1865 an ancestor of the present owner started the brewery, and long may the business thrive!

The lake spreads west from the buildings, dotted with green, bushy, nesting islands, where young willows catch the sun in their silver-green branches. The last hidden area of our central uplands now lies ahead. On the west the escarpment is advancing, and on the east the dip slope will soon lose upland character. But some high, wooded and little-known places remain, starting with Condicote.

Going up a steep hill from Donnington brewery we saw a local industry new to us, a trout-farm above ground, in tanks. An old yard contained ten or more green tanks, about 5ft high, covered, and linked by hoses from small pumps. A notice on the barn said 'Rainbow Trout'. 200,000 trout a year are raised here. We passed the first sign to Condicote in order to travel on Condicote Lane, or Ryknild Street, at the second. Looking back after turning I could see the old road continuing as a track straight along a field wall.

Condicote is a strange, quiet place. We went down a steep hill (of course) past a farmhouse and cottages, and came on a walled village green, with a good farmhouse at each corner, a fourteenth-century wayside cross at a well and spring, and a very small twelfth-century church at one side. One farmhouse is now the centre of a racing stable for forty horses from sporting owners and breeders all over the Cotswolds.

We took Ryknild Street again out of Condicote to the north, on a wonderful journey over the wolds towards Hinchwick and

Blockley. First the Roman road, straight, old and narrow, up and down, the wolds moving while you hold steady,

> . . . constant as the northern star
> of whose true-fixed and resting quality
> there is no fellow in the firmament.

Then, your resting quality beginning to fail, on to a roaming English road that brings the beauty of the deep dell of The Warren woods, and the roll of Bourton Downs that are quite different from wolds and rise almost to 900ft.

We crossed the A424 Evesham-Stow road and turned right on to the A44 along the front of Bourton woods, then left along their edge to Blockley Downs. Down, down we gently ran, skimming like the crows in the air. The orange-coloured tower of Blockley church showed up, and we followed it into Blockley, turned left beside it, and stopped.

This very curious place is in two parts. One lies round the crossroads by church and pond as usual, the other on shelves on the hillsides following the stream back into Dovedale woods. Round the church and to the left is an immensely deep cleft with a swift stream at the bottom, a thread of the Knee brook. On this there used to be six silk mills, employing up to six hundred country people. This meant wages, and gave a rural-industrial character to Blockley itself. The High Street is on a ledge above the cleft, and as you look across, you see houses built down the cleft-side in front of you and terraced up the steep rise behind, so that looking through arches and alleys you see sometimes steep garden paths and sometimes steep indoor passages. In High Street, cast-iron and pillared shop-fronts, mixed in with houses, are dated 1732. Here also are the *Crown Hotel* and a fine Baptist chapel of 1835. Donkey Lane creeps along behind the cottages down the cleft, to cross the stream and climb along the green hillside opposite. From here you can see the whole village laid out in crowded ledges, small terraces that were workshops in 1800, cottages, chapels, halls and schools. The silk mills on the water, each with a breathless lane down to it, each poised at a different angle over a big pond,

A feeling for town building: *top* A street in Northleach. Three houses, different in age and style, blend naturally. On the left the upper storey is raised behind a parapet with a good chimney; in the middle, deep gables combine with long windows, perhaps for weaving, and on the right are a dormer window, stone course and cut-stone front; *bottom* Wotton-under-Edge has saved its Market Street. Threatened cottages have been restored or made into the arched, cobbled entrance to an extension of the Swan

South sun on Chalford, a former cloth-working village spread along the northern side of the Golden Valley. The road and rail lines coming off the high ground down into the valley pass near the big house to the left have, of course, been converted into rare houses or restaurants, with good trout fishing.

The little centre by the church has a line of old mill-houses and a bowling-green facing the pond, a garage and dovecote in local stone built in 1957, fitting admirably into the traditional groups round it, and the old manor house opposite. Blockley leaves one with a very clear impression that it likes the way it lives, and has lived, and as far as possible it will keep right on doing so.

We turned back now to one of my favourite villages, Bourton-on-the-Hill. Old quarries mark the turn left on to the A44 for Bourton, and stretch far back, with Quarry Cottages to speak of the past. At the top of the village's hill is a beautiful eighteenth-century inn, the *Horse and Groom*. Here we stood and looked, and looked, and looked into the close-woven beauty of England, down the little street, over the roofs to the blue and green wooded wolds, levelling out on the dip-slope beyond the spire of Moreton-in-Marsh to the Oxfordshire plain and the distant downs.

Bourton-on-the-Hill street is golden and buff. The church stands on one of the level patches, and the post office and shop on another. There is a Sunday school dated 1828, very early, in the revival of faith after the rational, revolutionary eighteenth century; and a simple and peaceful row of almshouses, of the same time, when there was no old-age pension, nor organisation to provide it. The Norman church, perched over a drop, has coronation gates, terrific gargoyles along the nave exterior, a grey-silver east window with touches of colour, and Winchester bushel and peck measures by the lectern. All down the street on each side the cottages are delightful and well cared for, some sunk below the pavement, some up on stony ledges. All were built from stone dug in the parish, all speak of a quiet mind and firm spirit.

Just beyond the end of the village is one of the finest barns in the county, dated 1570. Built with seven bays, it has a gabled porch on each side, with wide-arched entrances for the mighty ox-waggons of harvest. The roof is of Cotswold stone, and sixteenth-century timber still supports it. The initials R.P. are cut for Richard Palmer who had it built. This also, with the almshouses and the Sunday school of 250 years later, is our tradition.

For love of local feeling, we made a detour here to see the Four Shire Stone on the A44 the other side of Moreton-in-Marsh. Past the big layout of the Fire Service Technical College, close against the hedge, within a railing full of creeping buttercup, a moulded base and square column hold up a gilded ball. On the sides of the base are cut Gloucestershire, Warwickshire, Oxfordshire, Worcestershire, for once four counties met here. The first three still do, but the detached portion of Worcestershire that made the fourth has gone long ago.

A regional piety fulfilled, we went back to Moreton, up the main street and off left to Batsford. Here, approaching the big Batsford estate and famous gardens, a herd of Channel Islanders was grazing in the sun at Boram Home Farm, buff-brown in the bright grass. This is Wychwood country again, spreading from Burford to link up in old days with the Woodstock forests – country of wild men, wild women, witches and enchantments; great hunting wilds for the hungry, the holy and the reckless. One still feels a strangeness.

We crossed the Knee brook again into Paxford, and swung back on a solitary road to Aston Magna, making for Moreton-in-Marsh, this time not to pass it by but to stop a while in this nice little town. I saw a field of strawberries in flower, and thought of South Cerney, where wonderful strawberries grow.

We struck across from Aston Magna to the Foss Way by Dorn, where there was probably a Roman fort in the first century AD. From here, the line of the early nineteenth-century Stratford & Moreton tramroad comes in beside the Foss Way on the east, and runs all the way to Moreton station-yard. Here the tramroad cottages and warehouse are in good condition. Two big stone pillars stand near them at the yard entrance. To my delight they were flying the English flag of St George, with the Welsh and Scottish flags and the Union Jack. Shouldn't we all equally enjoy mutual English, Scottish and Welsh diversity in unity?

90

Moreton is an eastern entry into the Cotswolds. A stone town, it stands on level ground, above the two streams of the River Evenlode, with the Foss Way running right through it as its High Street. The Romans had a Foss Way camp here and the road, built by 47 AD, has been in use ever since. Moreton was a handful of turf and wooden cots until it was picked on for the site of a new town. The abbot of Westminster owned the land, and decided to make use of good transport on the Foss Way. So new Moreton was built between 1222 and 1246 by Abbot Richard. This new town lies round the present church, and is now called the Old Town. The High Street is wide, with trees and a green strip and one or two old buildings down the middle, parking space and broad pavements. No hotel or bank or house appears more than three storeys high, and most buildings have only two, so that the centre is full of light and air and fresh breeze. The Town Hall, or Redesdale Hall, stands in the middle and pulls the whole scene together. The architect of Batsford Park built it in 1887.

The Curfew Tower, on the corner of High Street and Oxford Street, is the oldest building known in the town, probably sixteenth century, but I have never been able to see inside it. It has outside a copy of the 1905 market tolls. Beautiful eighteenth-century building continues on both sides down the street, notably The Steps, which has pretty gables, cornice and parapet, and really lightens up its surroundings. Further on is the *Manor House Hotel*, dated 1658, and opposite, a lovely row of cottages with brick cobble pavement.

What made Moreton a town was the presence of transport, first the great road for 1,700 years, then the horse-drawn tramroad to Stratford-upon-Avon, opened in 1826, and then the main railway from London, on which Moreton station was opened in 1853. It is very much a travellers' town, with good shops, restaurants, antique shops, bed-and-breakfast places, hotels, and The Swan Press and bookshop, most of them on the High Street. Oxford Street, off High Street, is well worth your time. The Congregational Chapel is open to visitors and the foot-weary. It is reflective and restful. I studied the Cotswold Sunday Schools' Scripture Examination Scholars' Shield of

91

Honour. Yes, indeed, it was up-to-date. Place names of the Sunday school scholar winners were round the edge, and included such tiny places as Cutsdean. A Christian could not but be gay in such a jocund company.

I was glad to see that Moreton had won the Bledisloe cup, the Gloucestershire award for the best-kept large village. Morris dancing is still a springtime pleasure in the streets and its big Agricultural and Horse Show in summer is the show day for the Poll Hereford breeders of Great Britain. This is a real day out for every kind of country skill and occupation.

Now, straight down a beautiful open stretch of the great Foss Way to Stow-on-the-Wold, 'where the wind blows cold', though we came into it on a June morning when the air was soft and the streets shone golden and brisk. Like Moreton, this was a market settlement deliberately planned by the lord of the manor, the abbot of Evesham, in the eleventh century, where three roads met at the Foss Way. The centre now is the market square by the church, in a small triangle of big roads. Stow has used this layout to keep traffic only one way in the little square, which is therefore pleasanter to walk about in. This and old streets off it have seventeenth- and eighteenth-century stone buildings, some gabled, some plain, with neat or fine chimneys, stone lintels and doorways, flagged passages and yards, all of the warm, golden stone of the county.

In the market square is the old cross, the plinth of which is one uncut stone. The church and old grammar school, 1594 (very small), are set in a quiet, green spot where the noble tower and tall trees give a lift to the simple square. The church, St Edward's, is of the twelfth century and most later centuries and seems to be a part of this century too. A record of the Chamberlayne family from 1706 to 1914 brings before you a thread of English history. The last battle of the first Civil War was fought in Stow in 1646, when Parliamentary troops under Sir William Brereton defeated Sir Jacob Astley, and 1600 prisoners were held in Stow church.

The other big building in the square is St Edward's House, which holds the town library, museum, and little art gallery; it is a centre for town life. Stow has catered for travellers since the

Romans came this way, and inns and hotels are a notable part of the Stow streets. The well of the spring used by the Roman camp is a 12ft stone trough down Well Lane, a leafy, quiet walk, looking over the Evenlode valley. On the way to Well Lane a tower rises over a garden wall; it is the top of a greenhouse built to match the nearby church tower!

In Church Street are the almshouses, founded in 1475 under King Edward IV. In Digbeth Street at the other end of the square, as I came out of a very good bookshop, a passing man pointed out the old, low, timbered house opposite as 'the oldest property in Stow', and it looked it.

Digbeth Street leads into a pretty green with a big, seventeenth-century house, a glowing copper beech, oak and holly. At the corner of Park Street and Union (ie workhouse) Street, is a hexagonal, two storey toll-house, another measure of transport. Beyond it is Enoch's Tower, four-storey, now a museum. Sheep Street, by its name, is early Stow. Glimpses up passages show interesting yards and work-places older, or less altered, than the street face.

Stow's most lively events are its two horse fairs, held in May and October each year. I like October best. Caravans with lace curtains and high steps crowd the square, horse-boxes jam the traffic. Down the road to the fair the yelling begins. The verges are a secondary sales site, without auctioneer's rules. Last time I saw links of unshod ponies, a stand of twelve donkeys, a grey horse with a child of three sitting with it, and a suspiciously beautiful black pony being led up and down in silence, probably without a log book. In the field, loose mares wander about with foals. Men wear long hair and high-heeled boots and alarming expressions, women are neat and slaves to the horse. In a dip by the gate, caravans, carriages, light carts and an acre of driving- and riding-harness are sold, at a rate an onlooker couldn't follow.

Grey Connemara mare, black Shire, Welsh ponies, steeplechasers, quiet-to-drive horses old and young – the auctioneer starts yelling the next one as soon as he has finished the last. A group of woolly foals, too young to be scared, were pushed in, stood gazing prick-eared at the crowd. One, to see better, reared up and fell over backwards on to the rest. A large man climbed over the rail, put both arms round him and heaved him right way up. Shouts from bidders in the crowd, 'Which is fillies or colts?' – more heaving, disputes, cries of 'It's animal magic we got 'ere', to the ecstasy of the crowd.

Children's ponies, exquisite little creatures hairy or clipped, were ridden by small humans or trotted by women. One was bought by an enraptured young boy for £22. A grave, seven-year-old rider exhibited a yellow pony, which went for £150. Perhaps the child went with it. Continuous yells from the auctioneer, 'sweet little pony!' The sun shone, Stow church tower was set over the showground against blue sky, the field looked across to bright autumn wolds and wood clumps. Across the road another field contained stalls and vans full of just what you needed, made while you wait, horse medicines, pickaxes and china violins.

The tour described in this chapter falls within the OS 1:50,000 maps Nos 163 (Cheltenham and Cirencester), 150 (Worcester and the Malverns) and 151 (Stratford-upon-Avon)

Golden Valley Country

To see the grey stone among harvest gold and orchards red and yellow, we will go where the wolds begin to feel the cleavage of the Frome valley that splits the Cotswold escarpment into north and south. The contours of the hills suddenly break up or are deeply cleft for a few miles, showing a little-known Cotswold character.

From Stow-on-the-Wold, run straight to Cirencester and take the Gloucester road (or Ermin Way) for eight miles to the left-hand turning to Syde, just beyond the *Highwayman*. This great road brings you close to the hidden head of the Frome valley – called Golden Valley higher up, Stroud Valley lower down. All the way it runs through wheat fields and pasture, swooping down and up between low stone walls, hawthorn hedges covered with traveller's joy in pale yellow bloom. Long, coloured views fill your eye on both sides, wheat and barley, green of beech and indigo of elm. The grey stone walls cross through all.

Syde and Caudle Green lead down into the hidden country by the head of the Golden Valley. Syde's little church and buttressed tithe barn along the churchyard wall are early medieval. The church is lit and heated by gas, the curiosity of gas mantles making them as liturgical as candles. On the lead lip of the font is scratched I.W. 1648. The old box pews could have watched the scratcher.

A real twister of a hill goes down to Caudle Green. In drenching rain I seemed to pass rapidly from the mode of knowledge of a land-dweller to a marine-dweller among floating weed and high rock tendrils of swaying green. The black-nosed sheep were scores of those seal souvenirs I brought home from Norway. Caudle Green is a tiny, up and down sort of place. A little stream where the road swings sharply to the left and uphill may be the Frome. The road leads straight

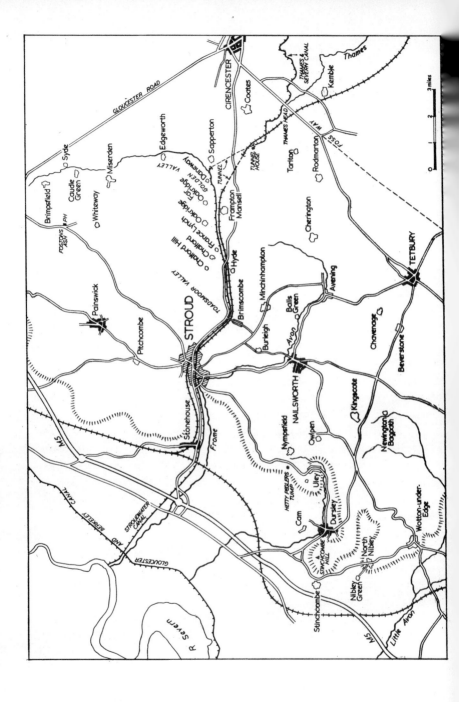

up to the country rising to the escarpment edge four miles to the west. Wet or dry, it is exhilarating, open, no roof in sight.

Old quarries show by field gates. The sturdy brown and gold of wheat stands wall high in two distinct varieties along the road. Plovers wheel and drop, swing and rise, calling insistently. Long, yellowish verge grass is mixed with blue harebells, scabious and geranium, purple knapweed, red poppies, and yards of pink willow herb.

A right turn onto a bigger road took us to Brimpsfield, which is said to have the smallest post office in England. The overgrown moat and mounds of the thirteenth-century castle break up the steep land by the church. A farm stands above both, and the castle ruins are generally full of young cattle. We searched out the lower stones of the gateway and gatehouse stairs, but most of Brimpsfield is built from stones of the old building, which has proportionately disappeared. The church is small and home-made; the central tower seems to have been too heavy and emergency supports had to be put in, probably by the castle masons. There are very old brass memorial plates on the walls, and in the chancel is a mighty stone tomb cover carved with a 9ft sword down its length.

As we went back past the castle mounds, a farm-hand and black and white dog were getting the cattle out of them, with some difficulty. The cows were freely kicking out at the dog. He took the laggard cows one by one, nipping their heels and jerking his head back to the centimetre required to miss the irritated hooves. We thought he would have his neck broken every second. But slowly he worked the whole herd up to the farm gateway. The man nodded at our admiration, grumbled at the damp weather being so 'waarm', and followed them.

The opening of the valley runs south-east for about four miles, with only Miserden and Edgeworth perched on the cliff-tops. After Edgeworth it begins a swing to the west which within two miles brings it round almost 90° to form the long nine mile split from Sapperton to the escarpment below Stroud. Although the Frome is a very small river, its speed and fall were enough to operate mills, machines and processes of many kinds. Other fast brooks rush from related clefts on either side. The valley lower down became the site of a dense and influential cloth industry, for which towns and villages were built, and canal and rail transport brought to serve them. So the valley is a whole unit, of deep interest to industrial archaeologists and all those who are interested in how people lived, built and worked. It is important to feel the valley as one; therefore we shall cross from one side to the other as we feel like it and as roads allow.

From Brimpsfield we passed over the northernmost reach of the valley at Glimperwell Farm and turned left onto the Birdlip-Stroud road, the B4070. The *Foston's Ash* inn marks the arrival of two side roads, one called Calf Way, while further on, down the road that forks left from the pub, the smell of new-made bread will catch you at the entrance to the former colony of Whiteway. Protheroe's bakery still stands behind the bushes by the road. We bought warm spiced buns there, though the man who sold them knew nothing about the place. The heart story of this colony can be read in *Whiteway*, by Nellie Shaw, one of the founders. Dig it out of your public library's reserve stock. A group from Surrey came, around 1900, in search of a place where they could live a life based on the principles of Tolstoy, rejecting all society's aids and organisations. The way of rejection proved no more blessed in itself than the way of affirmation. The colonists put up shacks in a region of good cottage building and lived their life by insisting on their own way to an extent no ordinary village community would attempt. Their children refused the ideas of the colony, and drifted away. No good simple building or art survives. The smell of new bread is all that remains.

Miserden, a mile beyond, stands on the top of the cliffs, looking down into the narrow opening of huge wooded slopes. Ernest Barnsley, of the Sapperton craftsmen group, built many Miserden cottages with their flat canopy porches. New houses are dotted among the old – but this village keeps its unity of character. A war memorial designed by Lutyens stands in a cottage garden surround outside the group of church, yew-arch, and copper beech, facing the vastness of the valley below.

Leaving Miserden, we went south towards Edgeworth. In a

field I saw a horned ram with four horned sheep. While I was looking at them a youth came by driving a small herd of white-faced horned sheep of most impressive dignity. I asked him what breed they were and he replied 'Dorset Horns'. Some harvesting had begun, and cream strips of fresh stubble edged the gold and brown. We took the left-hand lane that went down the side of the valley, past finely terraced grass hillsides, turned aside to see Edgeworth church, manor and vicarage group, then went down the 1 in 6 hill to Edgeworth mill. Our warm damp day was misty, with swallows whipping everywhere. The Golden Valley enclosed us in a tunnel of trees and silence. The bottom opened to a grass strip each side of the Frome stream. Across its head was the little mill, house and outbuildings, long, low and plain, backed by dark trees. It looked untouched by any but its original purpose and thought, an acre for Ceres:

> thy turfy mountains, where live nibbling sheep,
> and flat meads thatched with stover, them to keep;
> thy banks with pioned and twilled brims
> which spongy April at thy hest betrims,
> to make cold nymphs chaste crowns.

On hot harvest days one could surely pause here and see an older, smaller world.

> You sunburnt sicklemen, of August weary,
> come hither from the furrow and be merry:
> make holiday; your rye-straw hats put on
> and these fresh nymphs encounter every one
> in country footing.

Four bay horses were rolling in the mud just over the road gate, and scrambled up flecked with cream meadowsweet and blue geranium petals.

Crossing the Golden Valley, we climbed up through the woods, turned right onto the top road, and made for Sapperton. This is a complicated area if you want to see all its treasures, Thames Head, the canal tunnel at both ends, Coates and Sapperton itself. There are plenty of ways to roam here, and I am choosing one that takes you less directly but more revealingly. Here begin woods that link the Golden Valley area to Cirencester Park. The tops of all the rises were harvest golden-brown, shining among copses of green and indigo. Keep on past Park Corner and past the turning to Sapperton where the woods come close. Cross the great railway tunnel, in woods, cross the Stroud road (A419) at Chapman's Cross heading for Churnhill, turn left at Churnhill and left again for Tarlton. The road keeps gently level at about 500ft, though the flowing succession of wold crests gives an impression of being much higher. Near Tarlton the feeling of a village begins. There is a bright green potato field, holly and yew in the hedges, masses of blackberries and yellow travellers' joy. From Tarlton take the lane marked to Kemble, under the elm avenue. On this lane you can see perhaps the purest Cotswold landscape, delicate contours against a soft sky, the restraint of a thin soil, the stone walls and light colour shades of the limestone foundation.

We turned left onto the Foss Way to see ahead the *Thames Head* inn. Past this, down the dip and beyond the railway bridge, a gate on your left opens to a footpath across a small field to the source of the River Thames. This is variously described by pilgrims as a sheet of water and completely invisible. I expect the answer is in the season of the year, for here you are looking at a source of springs, not at a flowing stream. A stone marks the place. The statue of Father Neptune, usually known as Father Thames, made about 1855 by R. Monti, has been removed to Lechlade after damage by vandals. A little further along the Foss Way, the old bridge that carried the road over the Thames & Severn Canal, which has come here from Inglesham, bears a memorial plaque. Below it on the left is the old Foss Bridge wharf house. You can go down past this to the towpath, under the present road, and walk to where, beside the path, is the huge well from which water was once pumped by steam engine into this summit level.

To see the mighty canal tunnel and its attendant pub in the deep woods, take the next turn left off the Foss Way, to Coates.

This was a day's outing and picnic never missed in summer holidays when I was a child at South Cerney. We biked past Coates, round the left turn to Tarlton, and down towards the railway, hoping to see a great express rush through the fields with long flare of steam. The old canal round-house showed up, then a U-turn under the bridge, and we saw the overgrown line of the canal, the woods, the sign to *Tunnel House*, and the tree-tunnel to it.

But before going up the track to the tunnel, walk down the road slope to the bridge under the trees and look over the parapet into the dark, ever-shaded canal cutting. Then go up the track signposted to *Tunnel House* and follow the top of the cutting to the tunnel mouth. We always scrambled down the steep side, to stand dwarfed at the tunnel entrance, and stare into the blackness. It was built, in classical dignity, between 1784 and 1789 by Robert Whitworth, a fine Brindley-trained engineer. It is over two miles long, its bore 15ft 4in high and 14ft 4in wide, longest of known canal tunnels in Europe when it was built, a great engineering achievement in the days when people admired great things. The other end is at Daneway below Sapperton. The last trading-boat went through on 11 May 1911. Falls of stone and earth inside the tunnel have occurred since, and blocked it.

Tunnel House has been rebuilt following a fire, but it still looks as a Cotswold country inn should, and is immensely popular with locals. A field path links the pub to Tarlton by a walk through the harvest. Once we picknicked in the field after the bales were carried, with the harvest-moon rising pink and clear, and we could just make out the movement of deer stepping out into the stubble from the edge of the woods. This is the season for making rook pie and pigeon pie, when these fellows are gorged with harvest grain. Shin of beef, belly of pork, sage, onions, good short pastry and six fat young rooks!

Coates is one of the villages built or grown on a square, with an arm down a hill to the church. The tower of Coates church is to me the most graceful of any Cotswold village. While Northleach tower shows you power, Coates speaks of everything winning and desired. Seen across the fields, perhaps

101

through a scatter of rain in the sunlight, it will stay with you when you are far away. The last time I was there, looking at the fearful carving on the south-west angle of the tower of an anthropophagus swallowing his victim, there was a piercing shriek behind me. I jumped a foot, and turning round saw a peacock on a tall headstone under a yew tree, its tail sweeping down to the ground.

We took the Sapperton road out from Coates, through Lord Bathurst's farming and wooded land on the right, into thick shade of woods where the Bathurst sawmills are sited, onto the Stroud road and quickly forked right off it round the edge of woods to Sapperton. Here, instantly, a glory in Cotswold pattern opens. You are up high on a narrow road, close-sheltered by woods on your right, and you see the wolds displayed in glad confident character for a dozen miles away on your left and ahead, all contours blending into the light, airy sky. Soon, the canal-tunnel's spoil-heaps show in a line on the left of the road, each topped with beeches.

Sapperton is a village famous in the history of crafts and of engineering. It is sited on the cliff blocking the way into the Golden Valley which had to be pierced by canal and railway tunnels. The craft fame of Sapperton comes from a group of men who settled here at the turn of the nineteenth century when the social and personal evils of mechanised industrialism had been perceived but not tackled. The leader was Ernest Gimson, an architectural student who had been inspired by William Morris's creative ideas. Ernest Barnsley worked with Gimson, and Norman Jewson and Sidney Barnsley were also young architects. They all believed, as Gimson did, that creative work, preferably hand-work, in stone, wood, iron, plaster, wool, cooking, for an adequate wage certainly but for the joy of the work was the best means to personal fulfilment and social health.

Most fortunately, Norman Jewson, who till his death in 1975 still lived in Sapperton among the houses which he built or improved, wrote an illustrated book *By Chance I Did Rove* on the whole Gimson period and work at Sapperton. This was reprinted (privately) in 1973, and gives a sublime local account of the settlement and its lasting influence. Norman Jewson himself was later responsible for the repair of the great tower at Magdalen College, Oxford.

Sapperton nests above the fall-away of the deep valley. The cottages, singly or in groups on ledges of level ground, are small, stone and stone-tiled, with snug gables over little windows that face the huge drop and the winter gales roaring up from the Severn estuary. The little school, four gabled, is perched over the drop. On the Green are houses developed a little more fully through the eyes and hands of men with an architectural vision of the place. In the Glebe, and up at the top, are new houses. Sapperton is ringed with woods. From the upper entrance of the village you catch glimpses of tracks through them, all open to walkers or riders. Drop in to the *Bell Inn* for a sandwich and a game of bar billiards.

The church was partly rebuilt in the first years of the eighteenth century. Here is the tomb of Sir Robert Atkyns who died in 1711, author of the *Ancient and Present State of Glocestershire*. Here too in the churchyard are the graves of Ernest Gimson who died in mid-career, and of Ernest and Sidney Barnsley. Round them are others bearing brass memorial plates beautifully engraved, many by Gimson and his friends.

To see the other end of the canal tunnel, and Daneway House, take the Daneway hill down from the crossroads in the village. A formidable hill, high-banked, through thickets rich in native plants and insects. The old path for canal horses goes off to the right through the bushes to the tunnel mouth. At the bottom we paused on a narrow bridge of the canal days. On the left is a space where the wharf and its surviving cottage once served their quiet trade, the outline of a former reservoir below. From here one can walk down to Chalford beside the ruined locks. On the right the lock has been filled in for a car park for the *Daneway Inn*, once the *Bricklayers Arms*, and contemporary with the canal. You can walk from here along the towpath to the other dark opening of the tunnel, then either return to the inn, or up the horse-path to the road. Up the hill to the right behind the inn is Daneway House, which dates in part from 1250. Some sections can be seen by prior arrangement.

We went back up again to the Sapperton crossroads and took the turn to Frampton Mansell. The road coasts along the brink of the valley, passing over the railway tunnel and keeping above the main line in the deep Frampton cutting, then twisting down to Frampton Mansell at the *Crown*. This is another hill village, cottages built by Gimson men, all simple, sturdy and part of their setting. The gardens too, such deep-hung rows of peas, such brilliant scarlet and green rows of beans! At this season the huge valley over which they hang is mild and sheltered, seemingly beneficent to gardens, and hedges are thick with honeysuckle and traveller's joy.

We now left the upper world and descended past the *Crown* to seek the road to Oakridge across the valley. Down through woods and clearings, little level patches where a sheep and donkey or a couple of cows graze, or jumps for ponies stand crookedly, we passed under the railway, where a once good house has been almost encased by the railway viaduct, and on through silent woodland to canal level where a lock and pond and stretch of lilied water make a sudden clear setting for Puck's Mill house. Through a narrow green tunnel the road climbed towards the light, and we came out of the woods to see stone cottages, and orchards with red apples.

Within a mile of each other there are three surprising villages, Oakridge, Far Oakridge and France Lynch. They are all on steep pitches, some groups up out of wheel reach, with tracks of only packhorse width. The industrial ancestry of these little places is clearly that of the home spinner and weaver, depending on the regular travelling agent to bring materials and buy products for the cloth industry all down the valley – a most precarious existence. Now, they look prosperous, there is new building but not too much, and some very handsome houses. Their extraordinary charm is in being so pretty and snug in themselves, and so remote and unworldly. Employment still stems from industry down in the valley all the way to Stroud, but the inaccessibility of these villages by modern standards protects them from too much of everything.

In the eighteenth century, nonconformity took strong root in

104

top Stormy weather on the Salt Way crossing the 'high wild hills and rough uneven ways' near Guiting Power. The exposed landscape, dry-stone walls and the fine elm's ancestor would have been known to Shakespeare; *bottom* A lonely stretch of the White Way near Compton Abdale. Here the wolds roll with deceptive ease, providing open, high, dry, farming country especially suited to barley

top Early spring harrowing below the escarpment edge at Leckhampton. The quarry faces mark the great bastion of the Cotswolds looking over the Severn; *bottom* New Minchinhampton: The new six-sided annexe to the church, which uses the old skills as well as our forefathers did: finely graded stone tiling on the roof with its ball finial, and stone mullions in the transomed windows

the poor industrial groups, and Baptist and Methodist chapels are in most villages, big and well kept. Later settlements grew up in very poor, desolate parts of the valley, and these were in no church's care. Under the influence of the Oxford Movement in the nineteenth century, Thomas Keble, vicar of Bisley, gathered some young priests into a missionary movement for these places. Many churches were built and mission work was done. Oakridge church is one of these. Unlike the usual old Cotswold village church, it is high, light and plain, with a white ceiling and roof beams painted red/white and blue/white, and a pulpit white with painted panels. France Lynch has a beautiful church by Bodley, very tall on a sloping site, to be in one mass with the land. The interior carving and decoration are outstanding. So, more familiar, are the communion kneelers, a long panel stitched with village views and scenes. The dedication to St John the Baptist has encouraged hassocks which are very gay with the lamb and his little flag.

I remember the saucer-centre of France Lynch, with its houses on shelves and packhorse-wide lanes between; and the harvest in the vegetable plots, peas and beans, celery, all the root vegetables, marrows, brown-green onions laid out on shed roofs to dry.

From France Lynch we took the road to Chalford Hill above, and fantastic Chalford below, the first old industrial place of any size in the Golden Valley. The Oakridge pub was called the *Butcher's Arms*, but at Chalford Hill it is the *Mechanic's Arms*, an indication that a world has changed.

A road runs from Chalford Hill down to the valley, and on each side of this road, taking it as base, is a triangle made by two narrow roads which penetrate the village of Chalford Hill. Lower down, the pattern is roughly repeated for Chalford itself, but more confusingly. It is better to walk than to drive a car in either. The whole south-facing hillside was built upon bit by bit in the seventeenth, eighteenth and nineteenth centuries, as spinners and weavers, Huguenots and Flemings came looking for work from the mills and could get a plot of land to build a cottage and grow some food round it. A better-off man would build a bigger one. Often the stone was dug out of a cliff

107

side where the hole still remains and houses a car today. Any situation would do, the more inaccessible the cheaper. Slate tiles brought on the new canal after 1789 were cheaper than stone. Well-set chimneys, little porches, iron rails or scrapers, were part of traditional skills like potato- or pansy-growing or singing, which working men used without learning.

So you find Chalford hill and Chalford. Stone-tiled roofs and dormer windows are at your foot level on a path; over a low parapet springing with fern you look down into a back-yard plot and an old rose bush, phlox, carnations, parsley and scarlet runners. A cream-leafed maple leans over a dark roof. Paths follow a mazy way, opening here and there into spaces with homely groups of shops. From every point you look across the valley in air and light. Down towards the bottom, a spring and watering-place is set under a stone arch in the cliff wall, reminding you that horses once worked these roads. A Baptist tabernacle, a Sunday school, even burial grounds, are packed in. Big houses from the early days of settlement cluster on the lower slopes, built by millowners or clothiers, showing mature gardens and trees.

And so down to the valley road and the traffic, the old canal, the little river with stone-built mills, and the main London to Gloucester railway line, all crowded in side by side. Here is Chalford church, with work by Jewson and Hart the silversmith of Chipping Campden.

The lengthsman's round-house on the canal is now a museum. Only St Mary's mill is still working, though not making cloth. Industrial development in our own time has brought great pressure on this area for new use of space. But the Council for British Archaeology started a movement in which local authorities and societies have combined with industrialists and local people in an operation to clear dumping and advertising, open up the canal towpath, replant native trees, and maintain its essential character. The County Council issues a leaflet offering a guided walk along Chalford valley. After Chalford, as the valley runs down to Brimscombe, pressure on space for road widening and new factories has been allowed to have its way.

To see this northern valley-side in perspective, I like to leave the valley by the road opposite Chalford church, under the railway, and take the little road running along the valley-side higher up. From here you can see the dense, intricate character of Chalford on its wooded cliffs and along the Frome stream. On this road the only villages are Hyde and Burleigh, set into rough, terraced fields and steep lanes that lead to open turf heights and views. Much is common land, part of the great Minchinhampton formation, and loved for walking, riding and picnics. The landscape has attracted people to build fine or curious houses, Hyde Court, Hyde House, Upton Grove, the Ragged Cot faced largely in tufa stone. The road through Burleigh brings you down, past the *Yew Tree* inn in its commanding position, to Brimscombe that straddles the valley.

Perhaps the best of all views up the Golden Valley is from the level of Brimscombe church and school on a cliff ledge. One bright morning I watched men re-tiling the church roof, and a boy and a dog fetching the tiles in thirty-four sizes across a plank walk. Maybe the boy was not the Calculating Boy, but I am sure the dog counted the tiles.

Down at the bottom is the site of Brimscombe Port, where once Severn trows brought coal, salt and slates from the Severn for transhipment to the Thames & Severn Canal. Now, basin and canal bed are filled in, and new works have been built on them. The old salt house, cottage and brick bridge still stand, and one works is called Port Mills. On the road the *Ship* inn holds its origin in its name.

We reached the old towpath from the south end of the road bridge, through a factory yard and the space where the salt house group can be seen, and behind another factory. The path is shady and set apart, delicious with wild peppermint, buddleia and willows. I saw medallions and hearts cut in old house walls, and tiny attic windows above the main windows in deep gables, suggesting millhands or children. Across the valley are the grey houses of north-side Brimscombe, less crowded than Chalford. Behind the village Toadsmoor valley opens to the north. A man could start early on a summer's morning from Brimscombe, and climb to the top of the

Toadsmoor valley road and come out into fresh morning sun by the *Target* inn, while the mist still lay below in Brimscombe Port. This belongs in another chapter, but its character has made Brimscombe different from Chalford.

From Brimscombe we returned past the church and straight up the steep and crazy road to Minchinhampton Common. Roofs are on road level on one side, garden walls on the other. Suddenly we came out on the Minchinhampton level, where miles and miles of level common land stretch in all directions, and you can see over valleys to coloured slopes and woods one beyond another. The short-cropped turf is checked with pink clover, earthwork shadows, coloured cows, people and a few cars. Some kites are flying. Suddenly all one's weight seems to be lifted by the fresh, moving, lively air, the floating sky. This has been a grazing area and summer recreation place for centuries, and now all 600 acres are National Trust property. Of course, such a towering bastion was a settlement and camp to our distant ancestors, when the ditches and high banks of the common protected it against envious raiders. Not Minchinhampton only, but the surrounding country is noted for prehistoric sites, standing stones, stone circles, magical folk belief and practice.

At Tom Long's Post, five roads (and the one we came on) lead from the Common; one of them into Minchinhampton. This is another wool-and-cloth Cotswold town, though it produced as much stone as wool. A long, narrow, stone street leads into it, past old inns like the *Trumpet* and the *Swan*.

The centre is conveniently small, holding the 1698 pillared Market House and the *Ram* inn with its splendid sign, the beautiful *Crown*, Arden House and Minchinhampton Club House, and the charming, bow-windowed *Coffee Bean* cafe. Smaller houses among them, many with shop fronts, show the same skill and tradition. When I was there last, a saddled horse was standing by itself in an open shop entrance. A passer-by said to me, 'The horse is shopping'.

Good, traditional building was going on at the west entrance of the church. I walked up the path, and shall always remember at that moment hearing a shout of 'Well, I declare!'

and two old friends from South Cerney came out from the piles of stone, Henry Painter with his wheelbarrow and Charlie Carter with his stonemason's trowel. Their building firm from South Cerney was adding a six-sided ante-room to the church. The tiling was finished, and inside Charlie showed me a cedar ceiling, slightly shaped to the roof.

I went into the church and renewed my acquaintance with the great south transept and rose window, the brasses on the north wall of the nave; the fourteenth-century font, rescued in 1915 from being a flower-tub in a garden; and the young man who perished in the 6th flotilla of the Dover Patrol in the Channel in February weather, 1917. The leaflet told me that Matilda, wife of William the Conqueror, presented the manor of Hampton to a convent at Caen in Normandy. I wondered how many Minchinhampton men fought in the battle of Caen in 1944.

The town spreads out from High Street in close-built streets, a shelter against winter gales. It grew up as a cloth-making village, small houses with a big room for the loom, warehouses, inner yards, and plots outside the village for growing teazels for brushing up the nap. From Market Square, Well Hill dips down between beautiful seventeenth- and eighteenth-century houses. The curve of Well Hill corner into Tetbury Street is one of the finest pieces of mason's and stone-tiler's work, delicate and exact in the grading of stone- and tile-courses, so loving in the movement of the curve that the round corner lives and breathes like its townspeople, but in a different mode. A yard entrance has a monolith 7ft tall above ground for its gatepost. Did it come from some old barrow broken up by the plough? On a high, side wall in Tetbury Street one can still read in faded letters, 'Simmonds & Sons, Plumbers Sanitary and Hot Water Works *Laborare est Orare*' (To work is to pray).

I had read about the great stone-mines at Balls Green below Minchinhampton; spreading 2,000 yards underground in galleries and chambers full of bats. These have produced incomparable stone for work in Gloucester cathedral, the Houses of Parliament, and the finest stone flags for churches and wise men's homes.

111

Following the map we went down the New Road, through romantic country giving glimpses of beautiful houses, and turned down left to Longfords Mill. This was a mistake for Balls Green, but worth it because Longfords Mill is still alive and working, giving out that breath of life, the sound of looms. Tennis-ball material is made and exported to the USA, as well as clothing tweeds.

We went back and down to the pub on the valley road, the *Weighbridge*, a stone-built inn opposite the mill buildings. Photographs in the bar show 2-horse stone-carts. Here we learnt the way to the mines; a short way up the hill road opposite the pub, then a left turn, and by a path beyond the entrance to a small house named Box Lodge is a mine. The dark cliff face is obscurely visible, grown over and deeply shaded, the rough, rutted approach a foot thick in leaves, broken stone and rubbish. From the sunny path where we stood, harebells blue in the verge, I hesitated to go near. There was the feel of greatness, as at the entrance to Sapperton tunnel. The entrance is a half-buried cave, out of which creeps cold. Silence sings in your ears. The mouth is grated for the protection, not of foolish people, but of the precious bats who have settled a winter colony there. Of all the British greater horseshoe bats, three-fifths live in Gloucestershire, and many of them are here!

This exploration had taken me into a strange land, a mazy dance of high and low and round and round. The heart of this maze is Nailsworth. Nothing less like Stow-on-the-Wold, Cirencester, Burford or Chipping Campden can be imagined, but it is true Cotswold. Isolated, stone-bearing, stone-working, cloth-making, self-reliant by necessity and independent by result, this little world of miniature precipice, torrent and forest is English Cotswold too.

The road from the Balls Green mines to Nailsworth follows the flanks of the hill across the stream from the B4014 before dropping down to the little town at the junction of three deep valleys. Nailsworth streets rise up steeply from the War Memorial clock tower and the gentle, graceful front of the *George Hotel*, now rather dazed by traffic. Behind the clock the stream is bridged and leads into the sunny quiet yard of the six-mile railway from Stonehouse (near Stroud) built in 1867, now dismantled. 'Truck Loads at Colliery Prices' can be fadingly read on a wall, bringing back memories of steam engines and kitchen fires. On a road out this way is the cottage in which the poet W. H. Davies lived and died. All through the town, former industry makes the place interesting, like the clothier's mark of a ram's head and the date 1814 on the wall of a modern works.

In Market Street, delicate cast-iron pillars hold up many shop fronts. The hilly corner of Market Street and Fountain Street is made by the most charming clusters of houses and roofs close packed on the sloping land. We walked into Davis's Furnishing Store and found at the back a small hand-weaving business, with narrow looms and a range of desirable products for sale. A special spot is the Friends' meeting house of the Quakers, built in 1680. It is off Chestnut Hill, with a sheltered garden and cobbled courtyard. Many handsome houses of the seventeenth and eighteenth centuries can be seen on Spring Hill, built by clothiers and business men. In Cossack Square at the bottom the *Britannia* inn sells food and good beer.

The church is of 1900 and 1937, a light-filled place standing high on an island bank in the street. In some moments the interior is a shape of light rather than of wall and roof.

All Nailsworth's busy little streets look out over wolds and woods, or up into woods and sky. W. H. Davies wrote, perhaps here:

> Though I have travelled many and many a mile
> And had a man to clean my boots and smile
> With teeth that had less bone in them than gold,
> Give me this England now for all my world.

From Nailsworth we took the road just behind the escarpment edge to Nympsfield. There is new building along here, with some tile-hanging as a variant on the traditional use. The road climbs clear of trees to a gliding club area, and a glider towed by an aircraft often crosses the sky. We came down into Nympsfield at the *Rose and Crown* and the old malthouse, a group unchangingly attractive. According to established local wit, in Nympsfield

> All the people eat there
> is ag-pag dump.

This is a dumpling made of barley, nettle and dandelion leaves and other edible greenery, onion, herbs and eggs, all boiled together to eat with braised beef.

In the village a mobile library van, a copper sycamore newly planted, a footpath marked, are all welcome signs of the modern world. The little church and school were built by that remarkable architect Teulon in 1861; he was a master of simplicity and proportion and an artist in leaded window designs. Here the glass in these designs is all clear yellowy-green.

We took the escarpment road to Uley, pausing at a sign to pay our respects to Hetty Pegler's Tump, one of the finest long barrows on the Cotswolds. Hetty Pegler was the landowner three hundred years ago. What a road this is for summer roaming! Hardly any traffic, and you can see at any moment a rich green turnip field, a scented white clover patch with yellow butterflies, the gold harvest with white slash of reaping, a late unripe field, an orange-brown quarry and grinding machine and dusty men, the tall strong stems of hogweed like fan vaulting in green malachite, and behind all, beech woods, their pattern of spread branches resting on the air, and the blue sky now clear, now touched with haze. The tops of Marlborough downs show, forty miles south-east.

The road ahead shows Uley spread along the valley. There has been much new building here, but the basis of the old village remains in stone cottages, seventeenth-century and Georgian houses, Teulon's 1857 church and the *Old Crown* and *King's Head* inns. The modern bus shelters keep their tradition, with stone-tiled roofs and one with round, rubble pillars. This was a former cloth-working village, specialising in Uley blue cloth and black cloth. Remains of sheds and a drying tower and other delightful vestiges can be found.

Half a mile outside the village by the quiet stream is Owlpen, where you will find one of the most beautiful small manor houses in Gloucestershire. The whole scene is so undramatic, so personal, that its quality can easily miss appreciation. The house backs into a hill and a churchyard, and faces a stream, a field and another hill. But as I looked at the three crisp frontal gables and finials, the two flanking gables, the shallow broad roofs from which they spring, the varying, perfectly proportioned windows, I saw again a life rising from each line, the experience of love between designer, masons and stone. It is not surprising that, years ago, finding the house empty and the site unfashionable, Norman Jewson bought it and worked in it to make restorations. The house is open on Fridays in June and July.

The churchyard and church are on the bank close above the house roofs. From the churchyard a path leads to the lych gate, from where you can see the corn mill, with its lead cupola. The church has bold enrichments of inlaid mosaics, painting and an alabaster reredos.

From Owlpen our road to Kingscote was signposted '1 in 4, slippery in wet weather'. The weather was wet, had been wet all night. A man was cutting the heavy wet grass over the ditch with a sickle and long hook. But the sun was coming through and off we started. The car just fitted in between the verges, and tall campanula on the banks looked in at the windows. Beeches made their dusky tunnel, a stand with milk churns was set back on a farm turn, and then we came out suddenly on the top in the open. The Cotswold scene was again completely changed.

Broad wold tops on the main road and harvest fields concealed the clefts and hidden streams, the ferny dusk, the magical houses and millponds. We turned off the A4135 to Kingscote, a winding peaceful place of astonishingly beautiful houses and groups. I wanted to see again Sir Galahad in the church window. On the other side of the main road, half way down a big drop into the valley of the Little Avon, is hidden Newington Bagpath and its thousand-year-old little church, brother to a barn. From Kingscote we passed by Hazelcote Farm, crossed the A46, and entered a long, narrow lane to Chavenage. Here were huge fields and milking herds, a field of pink clover. A single beech and its shadow broke the silver sweep of barley.

The approaches to Chavenage House are confusing and impressive, long avenues and a mighty gateway in a seeming farm, a small cannon and shot. The house was owned during the Civil War by a Parliamentarian, Colonel Stephens. Oliver Cromwell and his general, Ireton, came here. The near-by Beverstone Castle was three times besieged during the Civil War, but Chavenage was not defended or damaged. It is open to the public on Tuesdays; Beverstone is not open but you can see a good deal of it from the road.

Aiming now for Tetbury we went north on the B4014 towards Avening on the Avon above Nailsworth. Avening was another weaving village. One of the mills remains, though empty, and a channel of the stream runs through the village. The old village is lion-coloured, down one side of the valley; the new village, row upon row of houses, is beige-coloured, up the other. I saw the kids in the old village go-carting down the street and steep dip to the mill, so I reckoned traffic was not a main consideration. A foot-bridge over the stream consists of one enormous stone. So do the gateposts of the churchyard, each some 8ft high. In the church is a monument to a pirate and highwayman, Henry Bridges, who settled here. There are two local collections of Avening concerns, one in the church behind the organ and the other open on Sundays over Millman's garage.

On to Cherington on a quiet road which becomes more and more hilly and wild, with patches of yellow toadflax and purple knapweed. Cherington has a lake, not just a millpond but a lake, in a dramatic, sombre setting that is strange in this cheerful little spot with its village green, drinking fountain, village hall, Drivers Charity houses, enchanting one-time village school, and pretty *Yew Tree* inn. I have been to Cherington many times, and there has always been an ice-cream van in the street. So I guess that it is a bright place and they don't worry too much about cooking.

No pilgrim in this region of the Cotswolds can be satisfied until he or she has passed through Rodmarton. Then you can wear the stone gable in your hat. For this is the place where Cotswold faith and practice have consciously combined to

116

produce a great work. Here, a big house and its dependent buildings was commissioned before the first World War by the Hon Claud Biddulph. The design was Ernest Barnsley's, and the Gimson group with the village men made the whole complex, cutting timber and stone, making the iron and lead work, and much of the cabinet work and furniture. Something of the house can be seen from a path off the village street. The skill learnt in the seventeen years from 1909 to 1926 when the great house was a-building was used throughout the village in cottage, hall and church.

The church contains tablets to the family of Samuel Lysons the antiquarian who discovered the Woodchester Roman villa and pavement. This splendid fellow, with his brother Daniel, vicar of Rodmarton, walked 19,503 miles between 1789 and 1800 in the search for, and the recording of monuments of the past, and published two volumes of engravings of Gloucestershire antiquities.

Rain and chill coming on now, we set off for Tetbury and the end of the day. The track of the former Kemble-Tetbury branch line follows the wold above the road, and Culkerton's old station storehouse is still there. We stopped at the inn with the curious name *Trouble House*, for revival and information. Revival was ready, for the house is CAMRA listed. The public bar is low, black-beamed, with window seats. A skittle alley is built over the stables. The origin of the inn's name is written up in the bar. During a nineteenth-century outbreak of agricultural violence against new inventions and machinery, rioters burnt the inn down (though the inn was hardly a new invention). It was rebuilt and renamed. And so, refreshed, we came into Tetbury with the evening.

The tour described in this chapter falls within OS 1:50,000 maps Nos 163 (Cheltenham and Cirencester) and 162 (Gloucester and Forest of Dean)

The Wild Escarpment

Tetbury is an open-air town with a feeling of the country round. It stands on a cross of roads, Cirencester-Bath and Stroud-Malmesbury, on open south-sloping wolds, well watered and ideal for one of man's chief needs, horse-raising for transport and pleasure. It has always been a market for Cotswold wool and cloth, and for country produce going south. In the centre is the seventeenth-century Market House on stone pillars and arches. Long, curving stone streets lead from it, all of a quiet, historical atmosphere. Merchants' town houses have been converted into hotels or business premises which are part of the busy and beautiful golden-grey streets. Most ways look out on wide country, some over a deep valley to the next rise.

All up-and-down Cotswold towns treat the problem differently. Tetbury links different levels by flights of steps alternating with green levels and open spaces, and houses built up beside the steps. The church stands on one such level, and its slim spire is a landmark across the wolds.

But Tetbury is near the great estate of Badminton, seat of the Dukes of Beaufort, and to Westonbirt arboretum and school. These two different influences have brought specialist knowledge and opportunities to Tetbury and its countryside. Farming, stock and horsebreeding, racing, hunting (with the Beaufort pack) and all field sports, deeply rooted in the Cotswolds, are more special here. The July Horse Show, the various horse and pony events, and the Christmas stock show are part of the life. Westonbirt arboretum brings top-quality specialists in trees and shrubs to the neighbourhood, and gives opportunities to observe and learn, which percolate through to local standards and events.

In another sphere, a main interest is music. Westonbirt and District Music Club is well above ordinary standards and has a

118

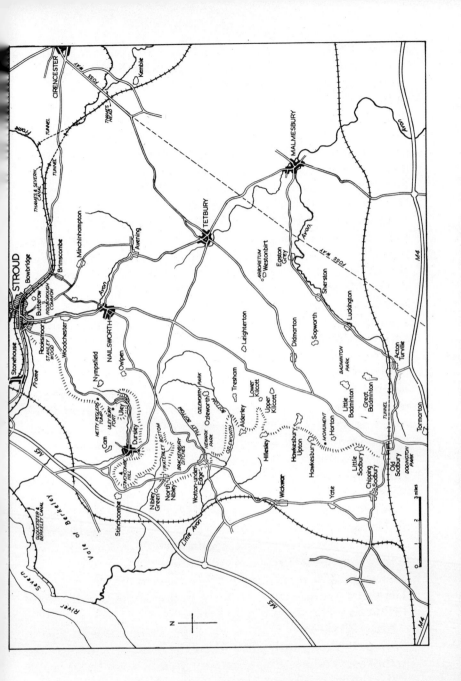

season of concerts. Tetbury church and Sir William Romney school make music in the town. One hotel has live country music every week. In August the Tetburians organise a time of public festival, costume, music, dancing, sports, and a good deal of feasting. Tetbury looks outwardly staid, but a lot of things go on. The town has developed a genuine, the-way-we-like-it character, which is unusual, comfortable and quickly felt. There is new building, some good, some very cramped. Between light industry on the spot and Stroud within reach, there is enough employment to keep the town prosperous.

Three miles out on the A433 is Westonbirt arboretum, one of the wonders of Europe. Apart from architecture, it is the most notable treasure on the Cotswolds – 116 acres of trees and shrubs. The original planting was established in the 1820s by Robert Holford, and has since been enlarged by 45 acres of Silk Wood, part of an original oak wood, a treasure beyond price as a naturalist understands. In 1956 the Forestry Commission agreed to be responsible for the arboretum, and now it is a centre of visitors' and students' attention. To ordinary people it brings a standard of beauty in delicately chosen planting for height and colour, or lowness and daintiness, rejoicing or reflection, which though entirely removed in scale from one's own possibilities need never be removed in idea from the mind. Each month has its own cherished blooming of beauty in bark, leaf, fruit or flower. 'Perhaps not to be equalled in Europe', the guide says quietly of the *acer* (maples) collection. The second week in October is the time to see this leaf colour.

Across the road is the mansion built in 1878 by Vulliamy for Sir George Holford. In a very modern way he diverted a stretch of the main road away from the hamlet, church and his new house; they are approached from a left turning just past the arboretum. The mansion has become a girls' boarding school. The district music club is centred in the school building, and Tetbury's horse show is held here.

After Westonbirt hamlet, we kept on by-roads to Easton Grey, a charming little place where the Bristol Avon runs close to the road, and weirs make a pretty curve of water by the bridge and a purely picturesque group of houses. You can see the big

120

house, once used by the Duke of Windsor, and its park dotted with horses. I stood on the bridge and watched people coming to the mobile library van, and heard the cawing rooks and the stream louder than they in the deep country freshness. Comfrey and meadowsweet were bright by the clear brown water against dark-red spires of docks, watercress and pink peppermint, and sunlight fell chequered through silver-grey willows. I would like to come in October and see the annual ploughing match here.

On down the road (B4040) following the Avon, the horse takes over and the verges get wider than the asphalt. We came into Sherston, which has its own race meeting. So does Didmarton, three miles across country. Stables and studs are frequent, horses and riders on the road, or training in the fields. Sherston is based on one long, wide street. Although so small, it feels like a little town. Its big open centre and quantity of inns and restaurants are clearly equipped to welcome race-meeting crowds or quality travellers up from Bath. The interior row of houses once common to all these wide market places is still here, and old quirks are appreciated – a grotesque mask on a house front has been matched with a new one; iron greyhounds adorn another; pilasters and patterns in brick another. Here 1683 is cut, and the *Angel* is dated 1648. The *Rattlebones Inn* (a local medieval knight) and the Anne Boleyn Tea Shoppe leave an agreeable impression of Sherston.

Crossing the wold towards Didmarton one is aware of the change in soil. The thin limestone of centre and north producing the contours, trees and plants peculiar to it has mixed here with brashy soil from Wiltshire. On lonely Cow Down Springs country near Sopworth, late marguerites and buttercups are rich, meadowsweet lavish – bright colours creep in tall thick grass, sulphur butterflies add to the gaiety. Is this not an aesthetic richness not truly Cotswold? Ah, but go down by the water, see the clear and gentle stream, the stone-arched road bridge – this is Cotswold.

Sopworth has kept a farm in the middle of the village. A real one, not an exhibition. It is set among good Cotswold cottages, all flaunting lines of scarlet runners and pea-vines, and the

121

brilliant dahlias of August.

The country rolled away on each side as we went on, small open quarries and barley fields among good pasture, dry stone walls bounding every field. As we approached Didmarton, we could hear the Bath traffic on the A433, which splits this poor little place in half. It is a pretty spot but for the traffic, with old houses, some washed a soft apricot and some with thick box-bush porches. It has three special features. At the northern entrance, on the right hand side of the road, is a holy spring and well, with big old stones round it. Since the Middle Ages people have come here to pray, and drink and bathe afflicted eyes or injuries. The second feature is a rare church, left unaltered since the eighteenth century because the local people built another one to use. St Lawrence's has a painted three-decker pulpit and painted box pews, wooden arches, medieval font. Among the scores of medieval churches on the Cotswolds, this is totally different. It is a treasure, but neglected like any unused outhouse, dirty, chipped, stored with boards and junk, in need of love and attention. The third feature is the annual point-to-point race meeting organised by the Beaufort Hunt, generally in March, a big south Cotswold event.

From Didmarton we turned south to skirt the whole splendid area of Badminton, woods and parks, the surround of the great house, the village and the church. First we went a short way along the main road to see Worcester Lodge, 'one of the most spectacular triumphs of the English genius for park buildings'. It is the entrance to the three mile ride which is lined on the entrance to Badminton House. What living spirit, what English balance and harmony, did the architect William Kent experience and express here!

The by-road between Didmarton and Worcester Lodge leads into Badminton grounds. One can ride or drive for miles past plantations, farms, little fancy buildings, wide sunny stretches of harvest fields, to Little Badminton, a delightful farming spot. Here also is the flying field, and the kennels of the Beaufort Hunt within the Deer Park. A left turn brings you into Great Badminton, a village that is just one street of cottages of all styles mixed in with some beautiful houses, almshouses

The wooded Golden Valley in shadow, and horses in sunshine, grazing near
Frampton Mansell church. Across the valley the wolds rise smoothly, with
beech plantation on the skyline

Old Minchinhampton: Retiling an old roof in Market Square which will live for perhaps century with the dormer windows, good chimney and drip mould over the gabled window on the left

of 1714, a village hall, shop and post office, all ending in the tall park gates through which is a right of way to the parish church. This path gives a sight of Badminton House.

How admirable it is to see a big area of country cherished coherently, consistently and with knowledge; where the land is productive in its capacities for food, materials, beauty and pleasure, with the future considered in its scale as well as the present; where there is a sense of worth-whileness in every part from field-gate to village hall, big house, little church and chapel. Part of the grounds of Badminton are opened for international horseriding events, including the tests for Britain's international teams in world competitions. So the place is even more a focus of interest than before.

From here we took the road to Acton Turville, the last village in the south-west Cotswolds. I have often heard of 'cottages ornés', but I don't think I could have pointed to any until on this road I discovered several, one orné with overlaying thatch held on timber posts to give a covered path round the house. 1898 dates one group.

Acton Turville is only just Cotswold. It has stone houses, some with stone roofs; a green, and a well on it, topped with a portcullis crest. A pub, the *Fox and Hounds*, shows photographs of sporting days of years ago, when the Queen was relaxing at Badminton with Prince Charles and Princess Anne as youngsters. Outside there is a three-sided toll house with a clock: swallows were feeding a late brood under its roof.

We went westwards to Tormarton. On no account attempt to cross the M4 – that Jordan is a final separation. Here on the Cotswolds' southern frontier a glorious view spreads out across the motorway – the Bath vale of many streams under a windy, streaked sky, and the rise of the Bath hills beyond, blue and green. On this side, the country is suddenly forgotten, little occupied, unnoticed. In its smaller fields and sudden rises, men were harvesting silver and gold, but the land seemed unmodern, shaggy, and put me in mind of the Old Men of the hill forts and tumuli on these rough steeps, where no doubt they watch and listen to the world passing.

Tormarton village is almost unknown, tucked in behind the

125

Bath road and the M4, with curious old houses and farm buildings. The church is a delight. A yew tunnel leads in to a proper country church, exhibiting every century from the eleventh. A brass with a little hare, cherries and a bell, more brasses under the carpet, rollicking marble cherubs, a cunning imitation of parchment in marble and Gabriell Russell's extraordinary tablet, must beguile you.

Immediately across the Bath road is the estate and house of Dodington Park, both of which are open to the public. The place is still occupied by the original Codrington family, who treat the public seriously, offering them interesting things to be interested in. The buildings are by James Wyatt and the grounds by that transformer, Capability Brown. The approach is through lovely parkland to the mansion, conservatory, stables, church, lake, children's adventureland. One can wander anywhere, and the estate is big enough to escape from other people's children.

There are three unusual features: the very comprehensive horse-carriage and vehicle display superbly presented in the stables; the open-air art gallery where local artists and craftsmen can exhibit from June to September; and the family historical records. I would think that this exhibition would give many people their first sight of the fascination of original historical records. Here is evidence of Codringtons as 'men of good note' in 1300, taking part in the first settlement of Virginia in 1607, founding the Codrington library at All Souls College, Oxford, and Codrington College in Barbados, in command of HMS *Orion* at Trafalgar, and sharing in history-making events from then on.

The road exit from Dodington Park leads onto the Old Sodbury road in steep and broken country and leafy lanes. Stone has been cut here for centuries, and deep quarries remain. Celestine, a rare mineral, is only found in Britain near Yate, a development of Chipping Sodbury. There are three Sodburys: Old, Little and Chipping. Little Sodbury has one of the biggest prehistoric camps in the west of England. William Tyndale, first translator of the New Testament into English, was chaplain at the manor house here in 1522, working on his translation (the house is sometimes open, by appointment). At Old Sodbury, the church is built on a steep rise, and you should make the climb and then go round to the tower end. You find yourself on a promontory: west and south the land spreads to Bristol and Bath. Go round to the north and see the Cotswold escarpment rear up in majesty at Stinchcombe Hill: the Tyndale monument is just visible to the right. Below it, Wotton-under-Edge spreads along the buff escarpment face in the sun; and beyond the escarpment lies the blue and green Vale of Berkeley and the silver curve of Severn; and still beyond rise the hills and Forest of Dean – England in her summer beauty.

A footpath leads from the promontory in amongst this beauty. Or one can go into the church and read a memorial to David Hartley, envoy extraordinary and plenipotentiary for negotiation of the peace with the United States of America in 1783. As we returned to the A432, we saw, near the *Cross Hands* inn, one of the crenellated ventilation shafts of Sodbury tunnel on the South Wales line, distinctive in being 4,444yds long. A little way along the A432, and we are at the end of the Cotswolds, at Chipping Sodbury. Yate, on its western side, is orientated to Bristol.

The wide main street, with its clock tower, is mostly two-storey, mixed and old. The stone is rougher, darker than in other Cotswold towns, but characteristic gables and good windows and porches continue. There is a Tudor town hall, a fifteenth-century house in Hatters Lane, and many old inns, as one would expect in a place that has held a market since the thirteenth century. Cloth and cheese were its staple wares, and many wide-arched entrances show their cart and waggon ancestry. Edward Jenner, vaccination pioneer, was apprenticed to an apothecary here. The *Beaufort Hunt* faces the *Squire*, whose sign is of a young man with an old-fashioned cricket bat and ball, a gun, horn and whip, racquet and balls, and behind him a rowing eight on a river. Good-looking restaurants obviously cater for evenings out for motorists.

Chipping Sodbury church (shut, but a notice said 'key at Mr Hobbs the butcher') is a handsome medieval building, and its special treasure is a rare pillar-pulpit of the fifteenth century.

The pulpit is reached by steps in the pillar, and has a pinnacled canopy with small fan vaulting, and a little window under which is inscribed 'Tobias Davis His Charge'. The simplicity seems to purge vulgarity.

From Chipping Sodbury, the country road through Horton runs almost without a swerve into the heart of the wild wooded country of the Bottoms, to Wotton-under-Edge. These Bottoms, which might in Devon be called combes, are slanting cracks running behind the escarpment face almost to the Nympsfield/Nailsworth plateau. Some have streams, some are dry, but all are deep, fertile, secluded delights, with the sketchiest track access, or none. Horton, Hawkesbury, Hillesley, Alderley lead to the opening of Ozleworth Bottom. Deeper into tangled country are Tyley Bottom and Waterley Bottom, journeys for a mad March hare on a May morning. The whole of this Wotton road is wild and picturesque; it crosses contours or swings round shoulders below hanging woods all the way from one out-of-the-world and delightful place to the next.

A copy of Tyndale's Bible is in Horton church. Upper Chalkley Farm on the way to Hawkesbury is one of the truly beautiful Cotswold farms. Hawkesbury's ancient church has foundations a thousand years old, and the manor court records exist from 1281. The group of church, remains of manor house, gabled vicarage and trimmed yews, seems to set time aside. Hawkesbury Knoll, too, is scored by terraces which might have been for vineyards but more likely were defence works of the Roman or British camp on the top. The monument, which can be seen for miles, is well worth the detour on a spectacular road. Who would expect to find the commander of a brigade of Guards on their Homeric day at Waterloo – Lord Edward Somerset – named and remembered here in remote Hawkesbury? The caretaker is proud to open the entrance to the tower and show you the record.

We came back from the monument on the road past Hawkesbury Upton and turned off left just where it joins the A46, to make a much loved, slow journey through Upper Kilcott and Lower Kilcott, by (naturally) Miry Wood and

Stickstey Wood. This is a kind of fairyland of small, intricate, comical and delightful beauties, including a nature reserve of marvellous soils, log-gardens, ferns, flowers and birds, in Midger Wood. Lane and stream wind through a bottom of green wolds, with small cottages, willows, and green banks where primroses shine in April and foxglove and pink cranesbill in August. The land of lost content must surely be here, round the next turn by the stream – perhaps by the mill in Lower Kilcott, where the house is dated 1739, the mill buildings are in sweet order, the pond is clean and full, the millrace fast, dark and foaming, and the old wheel still works.

Wander on in this land of pure delight till you come out at Hillesley, and on to Alderley, both villages in keeping with their country setting. If you turn right at the VR pillarbox, you will find your way into Ozleworth Bottom. This quiet seclusion has a lane only on one side, half way up the valley wall. It was a quiet, warm, misty day when I last walked there, leaves scarcely moving except with the quiver of little birds feeding on haws and elderberries, old man's beard and seedheads. From the green wall above me, to the floor of the valley where cows ruminated in a little stone shelter, to the green wall opposite, I was in a world where nothing was required of me, nature was at work, 'everywhere curious, articulate, perfect, and inimitable of structure'. All I needed to do was to observe and love.

At the head of Ozleworth Bottom is the entrance to the Park, through which you walk to the little church in the stable-yard. It has a strange, hexagonal central tower with windows and remains of loopholes. The entrance door has leaf-carving unlike any other, and you wonder whether some stone-worker from an Augustinian site in France had come over in the employment of Gloucester Abbey, to which this church was attached. The surrounds of the little place, and the stable block with its cupola, are a pleasure to see.

The prettiest way from here to Wotton-under-Edge is the lonely road past Tyley Bottom and Newark Park. This is all quiet farmland, woods, big hedges, or rough wold sides fit only for grazing. The Saxons called Tyley Bottom 'Tigel Leagh', or stone-tile quarry. It falls away from the road viewpoint like a

Swiss mountain valley, gentle, silent, individual, marked by trees and ragged hedges, cows and sheep: here and there the scar of a quarry or landslip. On the way to Wotton a footpath sign points to Tyley Bottom: that is its only access.

Wotton-under-Edge is a different Cotswold wool town. It is less composed, and has many oddities. Like Winchcombe, further north, it lies below the escarpment edge, but Wotton faces south-west down the vale. Many tracks and by-roads lead into its country surround, and above it rises the escarpment and the towering prehistoric camp of Brackenbury Ditches in thick woods.

There is an informal cheerful air, a rural aspect about Wotton. The main High Street slopes to The Steep which drops down to Dyers Brook, and then the road goes sharply up again, so that one always looks across to stone-tiled roofs, hearth smoke and changing leaves. Wotton was part of the mighty manor of Berkeley, so one would expect a medieval school foundation, church gifts and historic monuments, aids to scholars, charities for the old and for orphans, and a market. They are all here. More surprisingly it enjoyed the rights of a borough. High Street or Long Street, with the seventeenth-century borough Tolsey at its head, covers six centuries. It is the middle of the two main areas: Market Street, Green Chipping, the Rope Walk, Syn Lane, and The Steep are on the drop side, and Old Town, Pig Park, Bear Street, Back Lane and Tabernacle Pitch on the upper side. Market Street shows a welcome development. Several old houses near the *Swan* became dilapidated and were to be demolished to make way for a public lavatory and car-park. A local builder came forward with a proposition to save the old street, to restore and build in harmony with Wotton's traditional style and materials. This was agreed. A new housing-estate has also won an award. Here is a strong tradition acting on modern people to build well and refuse to cheapen their town.

Wotton is a place of interesting oddities. In the Rowland Hill Tabernacle (of a preacher, not the penny-post man) has just been constructed a facsimile of the Woodchester Roman pavement, the original of which can only be opened to the public at ten-year intervals, because of its site and condition. The facsimile, in itself a marvellous work of 48sq ft and 1½ million pieces, like the original, is open all the year round. It shows Orpheus charming all fear, anger and rebellion from great beasts and small, from birds, fish, trees and flowers by the music of his lute. A tablet in Orchard Street marks the house of Isaac Pitman, inventor of Pitman's system of shorthand, who began work on his ideas while a young schoolmaster here in the 1830s. In Church Street, Hugh Perry's unusual enclosure of almshouses and chapel is open to view. Down by the *Shearman's Arms* (listed in 1755) we had a sight of old working Wotton: small sheds, outbuildings, cottages, allotments coming down the slope to the ever-vital brook. There was the extra storey added to cottages to hold looms, and long sheds with a window along the front for apprentice tailors to sit in and sew. Beside the road crossing of the stream used to be the *Ram*, oldest inn in Wotton, said to have housed the workmen who built the church in the thirteenth century, with a footbridge across to the upstairs entry from the road. The sign is still there, but sadly, our favourite Wotton pub is now a private house.

As one walks round the town, one gets a feeling for those tough lords of Berkeley. Many of the family lived in Wotton and championed its concerns. In the church, north aisle, is the tomb and brass of Thomas, Lord Berkeley of the fifteenth century. He went with King Henry V to France and fought with him in the battle of Agincourt on 25 October, 1415, one of 'the few' of that generation,

> we few, we happy few, we band of brothers,

and lived to

> strip his sleeve and show his scars
> and say 'These wounds I had on Crispin's day.'

The church has a very special organ, built by Christopher Schrider, son-in-law of the famous organ-builder Father Smith. The vicar of Wotton bought it from St Martin's in the

131

Fields, London. Handel had often played on it. Over the south porch is a priest's room and old library, and inside the north door a water-trough for the shepherds' dogs who developed a thirst during the service.

Up behind Wotton is the Iron Age fort of Brackenbury Ditches, where I climbed on a sopping wet afternoon. Thick trees cover the circles of wall and ditch which form the whole crown, but there is little undergrowth and I walked easily in the green light and the silence. A fresh smell of timber working always seems to be there. At the edge the tree-trunks show the sky, misty with rain on my day, and away below shining wet roofs, and deeper in the mist, the Vale of Berkeley.

We left Wotton-under-Edge by the road up the escarpment, the B4058, then turned left along the A4135 for a mile. At Whiteway we plunged left, down to Waterley Bottom. Beech woods enclosed us in deep, gold wet twilight as we dropped down a 1 in 5 hill with narrow hairpin bends designed to ease the climb for horses, to a ford across the road, and then cottages and little farms in a jumble of steeps and bottoms. It is Grimm's country, fantastic, small-scale, operating on a purely personal basis. Tiny paths lead up banks to a door and low roof; iron work sprouts on many cottages, milk churns stand on tables in hollows; the pub is called the *New Inn* and it lies beneath Breakheart Hill.

Coming into North Nibley the return to a familiar world is gradual. North Nibley and Nibley Green are cheerful little places on the escarpment slope. Old building and some notable houses show a long history. The Tyndale monument, by Teulon, stands up above North Nibley village street, and an old cottage bears Tyndale's name. An inscription on the monument tells that he was born near North Nibley in 1484 and was martyred in Flanders (then part of the Spanish Empire) in 1536. From the top of the monument you can look straight across at Stinchcombe Hill, dominating this southern Cotswold country, rising sheer above the vale. Berkeley atomic power station, the Severn, the Forest of Dean are visible, and to the south the centre of Bristol.

There was a battle at Nibley Green in 1469, where Lord Lisle

132

issued a challenge to William Berkeley, and was killed in the resulting set-to, 'the local population watching from trees and vantage points'. Since then the Nibleys have settled down. Their big neighbour and employer is now Dursley. There is, I would think, not much change in its deep-rooted Englishness. The uproars of the distant world probably enliven the chat in the public bar of the *Black Horse.*

Stinchcombe Hill is the south-west bastion of the Cotswold escarpment, as Meon Hill is the northern. Stinchcombe village lies close under the hill, a street of plain cottages and some new ones, mostly up on banks above the road. Fine houses are built near, in estates planned to enjoy the views of the Severn vale, but the village, taking the first force of south-west gales every autumn, keeps its head down and shoulders protected. An old house at the churchyard gate, the school and the church make the centre. The church, like the land, climbs, four steps up into the nave, more into the chancel. The round east window has a light-green leaf-pattern that makes the stone tracery seem black.

The road to Dursley swings round Stinchcombe Hill. Foot-paths lead up to the commanding plateau at 700ft, all open space and wind and golf course. This rough hill country is alive with springs and streams, which once attracted mill-owners and engineers. Dursley is the only modern industrial town in the Cotswolds and there is interest in seeing how we do it here. The old town is concentrated along Kingshill Road, Parsonage and Castle Street, the church and market hall area, and, richest of all, Long Street which leads off beside the church. The first engineering firm that began Dursley's development was Lister's, and it is still here, making agricultural machinery and engines for electrical generating plant. Down Long Street you will find works, business premises and good-looking restaurants in among beautiful seventeenth- and eighteenth-century houses, some now used and well maintained by organisations like Lloyds Bank. At the bottom is the Priory, dated 1539, now Lister's offices, a lovely stone-tiled building, with gabled, two-storey porch and semicircle of old stone steps. I did not begrudge its occupation and careful treatment to the firm that has been part of Dursley since the 1860s. The stream and rushing millrace behind it keep a touch of old industrial character.

Older Dursley has much to show. The Market House and Town Hall of 1738 stands at the junction of Parsonage, Castle Street and Long Street. It is two-storeyed, on pillars, with dormered tiled roof and a simple country statue of Queen Anne. The church is partly built of local tufa stone, which seems strange to people like myself who know it as a stone for rockeries, light, with holes in it. The north aisle is longer than the south, so the chancel arch is slightly odd. I was looking at the glowing east window, which has glimpses of turrets and medieval roofs behind the figures, and wild flowers at their feet, when a local man said to me, 'Are you admiring our window?' His voice of love showed there could be only one.

From Dursley up onto the escarpment road, the B4066, all the way to the Stroud valley, is one of the spectacular journeys of western England. The road passes Uley, then climbs through beech woods and out onto huge, empty wolds, with Uley Bury, 32 acres of Iron Age fort, to the left. Beyond, it holds the escarpment as it climbs to 800ft. This is the edge of the great upward roll of the Cotswolds by Nympsfield. Down below, over the edge, Frocester Hill drops away to Frocester and Leonard Stanley, historic little places in the vale.

As we swung round the bend above Stanley Wood, mist thickened. We lost connection with the distance below and the wolds inland, and were held in the air, journeying blind through the mid-world of Niflheim. A row of about a dozen glider-bodies laid out on the turf by the road appeared as non-human inhabitants. We came out of mist onto Selsley Common, with beautiful stone farm buildings, and the Nailsworth valley opened on our right.

We turned right, left the edge, and fled down into the country, to Woodchester. Down in this Nailsworth valley, one is in a cleft between Selsley Common on the edge of the void, and Rodborough Common, though Rodborough itself is also the boundary of a greater cleft, the Stroud Valley. Astonishing variety, crammed into five or six miles.

Woodchester is deep down, haphazard, warmly enclosed by trees, and has a rambling section called North Woodchester. It is romantically pretty, with old cottages and houses in a charming curved street. Two men were road-training a lively, quivering chestnut, who, between the shrieks of a primary school playground, a yellow van and our car would have appreciated the compelling notes of Orpheus. There is one abandoned church, by the excavations of the Roman villa, and one built in 1863-4 by Teulon, with all his solid, lively talent. The memorial to Wedgwood Allen, RFC, shows a knight in armour with contemporary haircut and moustache.

The existence of Roman mosaic and stone remains under the old churchyard and in the land outside had been known at least since 1693, but the difficulties of excavating in a churchyard on the necessary scale were too great until Samuel Lysons' passion for antiquities overcame them. He began his huge excavation in 1793, and the finest example of a Roman villa then known in Britain was discovered; part was uncovered and the rest marked out. In the main hall was the marvellous Orpheus pavement, of which a facsimile has been made at Wotton-under-Edge. Lysons thought that all the million and a half tesserae of the mosaic came from the surrounding countryside – the blue lias limestone from the vale of Gloucester, white oolite limestone from the Cotswolds, dark brown stone from near Bristol, lighter brown from Lypiatt, red cubes from fire-bricks.

From the church we dropped down to turn right onto the A434 and then left off it for the madly twisting climb to Rodborough Common. This is National Trust property, and one is thankful, considering how close are fast growing centres which could spread housing everywhere. We came suddenly on a cattle grid, and rough country. Cows wandered from behind bush clumps and claimed the road. Again there was a Swiss note: the high space between two deep clefts – the Nailsworth and Stroud valleys – the simplicity of thin grazing, small humps and hollows, cows and the huge sky.

Rodborough Common has been lived on since primitive times. One of the rare finds of Iron Age metalwork was made here. After seventeen hundred years much has appeared on the

135

more accessible parts of the Common, a village, a folly fort castellated and used for occasional gun salutes, signals or fireworks, the *Bear* inn, a welcome meeting place in bleak months, the fine group of Stanfields Cottages with its Cotswold gables, oval and mullioned windows, and summer visitors from the busy Stroud valley.

From the top of the Common you can see the lower Stroud valley and the wooded south-facing slopes. Turn down the old toll road to Butterow and the Bowbridge crossing of the valley. You look for a moment over golden-green beeches, and then wind down through layer after layer of their beauty, the soft brilliant leaves extended in endless clear intricacy, the grey smooth trunks, the bronze of fallen leaves colouring all the ground. You pass the *Woolpack*, sign of old industry, the Methodist chapel equally so, a Cotswold stone bus-shelter. Old Stroud rises in front of you all the way. At Butterow you can see the toll-house and the list of toll charges for road traffic, hoof or wheel. Down into Bowbridge, over the river, the canal (this part now restored) and the railway, turn left, and you are in Stroud.

The tour described in this chapter falls within OS 1:50,000 maps Nos 162 (Gloucester and Forest of Dean), 172 (Bristol and Bath) and 173 (Swindon and Devizes).

Over the Hills from Paradise

Stroud is a mine of different interests: its industrial history going back to the late Middle Ages; its position on a stream-bearing split in the Cotswold escarpment; its architecture and social records; the crowding of canal, rail and road in the narrow valley; the vigorous life of a hill town somewhat shut away and the more lively for that, perennially keen on sport, tobogganing down the ice-bound town roads, hunting on foot and pony, racing and athletics on the level above the town, brick and rolling-pin contests with Strouds in Canada, USA and Australia.

The old road runs along the valley and joins the main shopping centre, King Street. In the angle between these two, the lanes and roads of Stroud climb up the valley side to join the lanes threading across this jut of the escarpment to Painswick, Cranham and Birdlip. A brilliant classical building stands at the opening of King Street and, as you would guess, it houses Lloyds Bank. In the entrance to the shopping centre is an interesting mural showing important local buildings of many kinds in the area, mills, clock towers and such. Near by is the very worthwhile Stroud Museum. This, called a School of Science and Art, was built in the 1890s, and is now a centre of knowledge about Stroud, the area, the woollen industry and any kind of rural industry.

In High Street, old Stroud still escapes the demolition men. Here the observant eye can see that iron was the modern material when Stroud was growing. The modern-minded man in the nineteenth century used it for shopfronts, lettering, works-entrance arches, girders for works and warehouses, all things which had been done before in stone and timber. Now, these are pieces to be looked for. Above the shopfronts in High Street you can see the older stone-tiled roofs and gables and tiny windows. Set beside a shop window, I saw a curious clock

137

which was a watchmaker's regulator, used to give railway time for the town in 1858. Up High Street are the Shambles, or meat market, with iron-pillared shelter and two original butcher's tables with knife marks. A craftsmen's market is held here on Thursdays, a big affair. The Town Hall, of the sixteenth century, faces it, and the church, built of Bisley stone. It was rebuilt in the last century and has especially good modern stained glass.

The fine Subscription Rooms, where everything goes on in Stroud, are in George Street. They were built in that perceptive architectural period, the 1830s. Beside them, in Bedford Street, are a huge Congregational Chapel and a little building on the corner, called Tucks, that was originally a very early hospital. On the other side of the Subscription Rooms is the old Cloth Hall, sadly come down in the world but still showing its lineage in the upper storeys.

I especially remember Nelson Street for old nooks and glimpses, and also for an Equine Boutique. The Stroud Building Society has another mural by the same hand as that by the shopping centre, making a design of the many old tokens used for money by firms or companies. At one end of narrow, dark Church Street is the vicarage, dated 1635, and at the other a lovely little seventeenth-century house with oval window in the gable. Indeed, there is something charming in every street, if demolition does not catch up with it. One surviving old terrace, Rowcroft, leads down to the railway and canal area, a treasure of industrial archaeology in spite of much demolition. Here is Wallbridge, the end of the Thames & Severn and beginning of the Stroudwater Canal. On the left of the road, one looks down into the last lock of the Thames & Severn, where there is nearly always a temporarily trapped swan. The Stroudwater basin on the other side of the road has been filled in and its company offices, now the Water Authority's, stand beside it. This building, with oval windows and sloping side wings, resembles the wharfingers' houses on the Thames & Severn at Kempsford and Latton, which were directed to be built in 1789. The huge viaduct for the old Midland railway line to Stonehouse and Bristol still dominates this area.

138

Brunel's original Great Western Railway station and approaches are beautiful, serious and stylish. What more can you ask? Clean Cotswold stone and line, fine windows even in working buildings and the loading bank, expressing the dignity and pride in work and industry we need so badly today. The station is the only one I know with a full-sized tree on the platform.

Stroud is the focal point of all the south-west Cotswolds, in education, employment, health, sport, and arts. It has a week's festival of music and drama each autumn. Football and all league sports are centred here, and the rough country is keenly ridden and hunted over by the Berkeley, Cotswold and Beaufort packs and their medley of followers, tough ponies getting as good a day as big horses. In the industrial life which supports it all, five old mills still produce almost as much cloth by modern methods as when over 200 were working. Stroud still makes the scarlet cloth for the Guards' uniforms, and officers' uniform cloth for the Army, Navy and RAF. The grand old mills, about which you should ask the curator of Stroud Museum, generally built off the road where a millpond could be fed from a stream, are a glory to the Stroud area. Many now make other products than cloth.

Most of the industrial traffic keeps to the A419 down the Stroud valley till it reaches the M5 or the A38. The A46 goes north over the top to Painswick and then past Prinknash and off the escarpment; the B4070 climbs north-east up the Slad valley and then keeps along the escarpment to Birdlip. East of these roads, behind Stroud, lies a little-known country, webbed with tracks of long occupation. It is one of the high-grade stone-bearing regions, ranking with Taynton, Minchinhampton and Leckhampton. Enclosed by the escarpment and the Golden Valley, it lives its own life, acknowledging Painswick as its capital, Queen of the Cotswolds.

I think the best way to appreciate this out-of-experience region is to leave Stroud by the valley road to Brimscombe and take the turn left to Eastcombe. Cottages of older industry perch above the road-sides. This Toadsmoor valley road, much older than canal or railway, leads into an older world. A stream

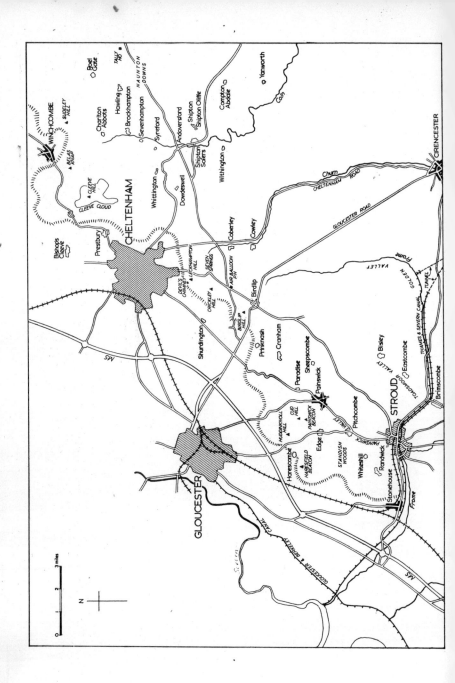

Minchinhampton's market hall at street level. This has stone arches and outer pillars and wooden interior pillars, all with stone bases. The floor is flagstoned

top Tetbury's eighteenth-century church with its surprisingle big nave windows, showing the line of the curious lateral passage that runs outside the aisles. Tetbury's steep land-base makes problems and gives charms; *bottom* The Devil's Chimney, a tall limestone curio on Leckhampton Hill above the quarries. The Chimney looks far away from the escarpment towards the Malverns

runs by it, woods crowd in, woodman's tracks disappear into them, one hears small saw-mills, countless birds, catches glimpses of inspired old houses on sunny slopes, chimneys, tumps and tumuli. Hidden through the woods is Bussage, where Michael Dinkel has his workshop, a glass engraver and stained-glass artist, member of the Guild of Gloucestershire Craftsmen. The road twists and climbs; a coach crept past us called Alpine Tours. A valley showed up below, with a timber-yard and saw-mills, and we came into little Eastcombe, hanging on the valley side. Here is a pub called the *Lamb* (it offered a fire and views down the valley), and a mission church of Keble's tradition, with a tiny organ by John Coulson of Bristol. On from the *Lamb* a 'No Through Road' sign led us to look over the drop where old grey houses and chimneys cluster on leafy ledges.

The road out of Eastcombe leads to a spring of beauty in this sheltered country, Bisley, a little stone town which has always seemed to me touched with some quality not wholly of stones and mortar. There is a strangeness in the style and mastery of its plain house and shop fronts on narrow pavements, in its completeness like an illustration to a lost book. It is very small, and everything is just a little more enchanting than one can believe, and yet, each time I go back to Bisley, the enchantment is stronger than before. Round it the area is rich in good houses and farming estates, and mission churches springing from Bisley itself. Older worship has been traced here, on altars dedicated to the god of agriculture, but to us it is known for the kindling of Christian teaching and worship in the many lonely cottage weaving settlements in the nineteenth century under the Kebles. Thomas Keble, father and son, were vicars here from 1827 to 1903, through two long depressions of cloth and agriculture.

The faintly other-world quality started as we came in from Eastcombe, and then turned down to the springs pouring from a cliff wall on the road into a low-walled basin. Here the dressing of the wells takes place on Ascension Day, a picturesque ceremony when the children of the village bring flowers and sing round the water. Then, as we strolled along the irregular

143

lines of George Street, High Street and Church Street, we were hardly aware of having slipped back two or three centuries, so at home did we feel with the native mastery of simple (not always cottage) stone design and building. Old things are not desirable simply because they are old, but when they have been able to mature, when roof and wall lines have slowly accorded with each other, and colours have passed, by weather, lichen, or the life of the stone surface, from single tones to layers of shades seen, lost and found. The old buildings do not attack the eye or nerves, but open and encourage. One feels related, and developed.

The *Bear* inn is Bisley's old Courthouse, and handy to it is the lock-up, two cells under a pretty gable where one could sit and chat. Outside is a milestone, an iron plate lightly scratched 'X miles to Gloster' and signed. Near the church is the Bluecoat School, and I walked across the playground under falling lime leaves to see the old Court and gazebo from the churchyard. Pale gold leaves and pale gold stone mingled together. The thirteenth-century church, object here of so much devotion, is a rich, happy place.

Another big house in the town is Over Court, associated with Queen Elizabeth I. Its fine gardens are opened in their season. The smith at Bisley forge is Norman Cucknell, son of Alfred who was chief smith in the Sapperton craftsmen group and worked on Rodmarton House. A toymaker lives here, Margaret Brown, award member of the British Toymakers' Guild, seemingly well fitted to the joyous character of Bisley in her world of little animals, puppets and tiny houses.

The road to Sheepscombe leads north out of Bisley past long barrows, and farms that show the excellence of Cotswold farm building. Past The Camp, we crossed the B4070, went down into the woodland, and out to the surprising landscape of Sheepscombe. Steep green valley sides run in and are halted by the wall of the escarpment edge. A little road threads each side and the bottom is left to sheep and scattered cottages. It is a sheltered end, and extraordinary stillness fills the gentle scene. Here the fierce gales of winter roar over the edge, above the clustered flock, the low sheltering barns, the close-gathered cottages backed into the contours on twists and turns.

> How blest are shepherds, how happy their lasses,
> While drums and trumpets are sounding alarms!
> Over our lowly sheds all the storm passes
> And when we die 'tis in each other's arms.
> All the day on our herds and flocks employing,
> All the night on our flutes, and in enjoying.

It must often have been so in Sheepscombe. A little church with fancy tower, a little pub, cater for local needs. The pub shows photographs of many sports, a notice gives details of the Harvest Supper.

We came now into the Painswick valley, a haunt of old times. Painswick's water brought the cloth industry here from 1600 onwards. One stream rises on the west from Huddinknoll Hill and one on the east above Paradise, and these two join on the southern skirts of Painswick. So there was water enough to drive many mills, and stone to build them in Scottsquar Hill and mighty Painswick Hill. Wide common land as well as private acres grazed countless sheep. Painswick stone developed a wealth of skilled masons to work it and learn from it. It stands in Gloucester cathedral, it rebuilt parts of London after the bombing, in Southwark cathedral, in the Old Bailey and in the vaulted roofing of the deanery at Westminster Abbey.

A succession of memorable mill buildings and clothiers' houses meets one along the valley. Skinner's mill and King's mill are expressions of belief, of a way of life based on work and personality. They are on a big scale, with well planted trees, stables with oval or arched windows and courses of pigeon holes, with iron sluice and stone clapper footbridge, the water runway built in a curving shallow stair.

We came into Painswick past long farm buildings and the Foxbury stud. The main road turns into a street which ends in the church spire. Church Square is the centre and round it spread the cream stone streets, New Street, St Mary's Street, Tibbiwell, Friday Street, Bisley Street, some hugging little neighbourhoods, some looking over roofs to open country

145

rising to sky-haunting Huddinknoll Hill. Church Square is graceful, varied, enchanting, substantial. Blacksmith's work is well shown in the old stocks close to the churchyard wall. The church itself stands on the site of earlier building, and is mostly fifteenth century, the more beautiful for being still and plain. It has had a lot of damage, twice struck by lightning and once attacked by Cavaliers in 1644 when the Parliamentary troops occupied it and the neighbouring houses. Marks of cannon-balls can be seen on the tower, north side, and on east and west church walls. Before the high altar and in the chapel of St Peter hang silver lamps made by George Hart, silversmith of Chipping Campden.

Gloucestershire has always been a great county for the music of the iron tongues, perhaps because of the bell foundry at Gloucester and its family of Rudhall. One of the oldest county associations is the Ancient Society of Painswick Youths, founded for bell-ringing in 1686 and still ringing today. Painswick has a peal of twelve. The ringing chamber shows lists of record peals: Cators, 12,006 changes, 7 hours 55 mins, in 1737; Grand Sire Cinques, 12,001 changes, 8 hours, 45 mins, in 1920. Throughout the county the local associations gather on Saturdays in towers by turn, for outings of ringing, meat teas and beer. Not only in the stately towers but in the villages for Sundays or weddings you may hear the bells being 'got up' and then moving into their pattern of sound. Christmas Eve, New Year's Eve, the clash and dance echo in the frosty night. Our family are ringers, and we hang out of the windows to hear the bells and watch the stars. This art, different from carillons and handbells, practised only by the English, is deeply rooted in the countryside, and the Cotswolds will give you many hours of it. If you are staying in a village you may well be taken up into the ringing chamber and initiated into the art.

The churchyard is as important to Painswick as the church, for its yews and tombs. The oldest yews were planted in 1792, and the saying is that there are ninety-nine but no one can come to the same number twice. In September, clergy, choir and children join in the Clipping Ceremony, process through the churchyard, join hands encircling (clipping) the church and sing a traditional hymn. The tombs, mostly table-topped, range from 1603 to 1841 as so far deciphered, and are a collection far surpassing any other in the Cotswolds. Hearts, ovals, sprays and ribbons, skulls, lyres, shells – all your fancy is here. A tomb trail is published, identifying many of them, their carver, work and lettering, and a Painswick group works on saving or caring for dilapidated tombs.

The little place grew prosperous from wool and cloth. Painswick clothiers enriched their town by almshouses, hospital and schools, and by their own handsome dwellings. No mean or ugly house would do for a clothier. More than that, the town, the outward form of public life, was part of the feeling a man had for his life and his work. It is to be hoped that the collapse of this feeling in our time, with an inevitable decay of people's care for amenities, will soon wither, and give place to new growth and energy. Our eyes have been opened to the value of small integral places like Painswick just in time before we allow them to be destroyed by neglect, or by the man, be he owner, planner or builder, who is moved only by money, to make or to save it.

The place hums with life. Lorries steer in and out of fine stone gateways to working yards, low-fronted gabled shops are crammed and busy, notice boards carry more than the usual stunning lists of local activities.

How beautiful Painswick is! What enchantment is held by confinement in these steep wolds! Winchcombe is losing coherence by straggling extension and neglect of its natural gift of a stream and valley. Painswick, far less accessible, is more striking. On a sunny morning the cream walls, dark roofs and scrubbed doorstones with black iron footscrapers have a visual tingle from the light-holding limestone cut and worked in endless patterns and shadows in porch, gable, moulding and pillar. When wet mists are blowing through the streets, the town glimmers bright, shapely, magic-holding. Busy little medieval cottages, meditative sixteenth- and seventeenth-century houses, bland and responsible eighteenth-century mansions, merchants' houses and shops, serious nineteenth-century houses, chapels and offices, with inns altered and

147

re-altered from century to century, make up a town enlivening and enriching to eye and spirit.

From the half-timbered post office to the new terrace in Vicarage Street, there is something delightful wherever you walk. In Bisley Street, the National Trust owns a house called The Little Fleece, used as a bookshop; and you can go in and see the old interior fully in modern use. The top floor is a weaving room. As in Minchinhampton, on one boldly curving street corner the whole tiled roof has taken life from the tiler's hand.

Painswick has a remarkable Institute, meeting place for the music club and many activities. It also holds the annual exhibition of the Guild of Gloucestershire Craftsmen. This association was founded in 1933 on the basis of ideas of Gimson and the Sapperton group. Membership is strictly selective, though there are those under 30 besides others of long standing and reputation. The Guild has influence throughout the county, and also on the 7,000 or more visitors to their exhibition every August. One of my own highlights was finding there a craftsman who designed and made for our house a fireplace and hearth of unpolished green slate.

After Painswick the country takes over from the buildings, and the high, stony escarpment dominates the villages. Painswick Beacon is due north of the town, 930ft high. We left Painswick by Gloucester Street past the almshouses and Painswick House of the 1730s, and turned left to Holcombe, then right over Cud Hill and on to Painswick Beacon (Hill) which rises between the Gloucester and Cheltenham roads. I climbed the steep foot tracks past dells of old quarries grown over with bending ash and rowan, slope rising behind slope, every ledge bringing new distance to the eye in low towers of old churches, roofs of little villages, dark woods and the silver Severn. The first green rampart of the Old Men's camp rises. There is a way through the triple ramparts to the summit. Here is sky and air, thin cloud, and generations beyond counting of time held in timelessness. The mind expands in the silence. On a still autumn day one can wander, lie on thin warm turf, see the delicate tough harebell at eye level, the outcrop of white stone, the darting birds.

148

The Beacon is the chief point of this stretch of the escarpment, but the chief among worthy companions. Away then, down from Painswick Beacon, on to the A46; turn right, and left in Painswick again, down to the Wick stream and the great mills, with substantial old houses on the slopes, along Steppingstones Lane and past Juniper Hill (what names!) until a road bends sharp right to climb to escarpment country, with Pitchcombe as first step. Hill road, hill village, Pitchcombe clings on a hairpin turn at the head of a fold in the hills, beautiful, tiny, wonderfully inaccessible. Either there isn't any ground or it has been dug out for stone.

You cannot cross the escarpment clefts, but must go along one side and back the other. On up the A4173 to Edge, with the sweet Painswick valley all the way on the right. New building, using the new tiles, here among the old. The Romans fitted in a snug villa farm facing south east on the steep enclosed rise to the edge. Leave Edge on another hairpin turn left to Whiteshill, with Haresfield Beacon blocking the sky on your right. Down Scottsquar Hill, which is like the first hill of the world's edge, blocks of stone in layers in quarry faces on each side, beech and ash clumps clinging to the sheer surface. Everything in sight swings up to the escarpment, shut in but seeking it.

Down through Whiteshill I saw not only the sweep of farmland but several new bed-and-breakfast signs and guest house notices of the kind which had disappeared a few years ago. At the *Woodcutter's Arms* we turned sharp again on a randy road to Randwick, whose cottages wind round the hill above a green valley in a swinging turn. The road drops steeply, winding through orchards here sheltered from the gales, and then narrows to the village street; walls hold it in from the drop, the playground is fitted in down below the school. The sturdy old fourteenth-century church tower marks another characteristic turn.

Between Randwick and Scottsquar Hill are Standish Woods, a National Trust property of escarpment trees and hanging beech woods, site also of barrow and tumulus. They hide themselves from easy access like the woods of Gramarye. From Randwick, Ash Lane (towards the NT sign on the Ordnance map) is the narrow way to reach them, and in this season of autumn splendour we followed it. Suddenly the woods blocked half the sky. Now we climbed a little to the muddy gate and looked over Stonehouse at the bottom of the escarpment, over the Vale of Berkeley to the curve of the Severn as it broadens out to Frampton Sand, and beyond Severn to the hills of the Forest of Dean. I turned back and looked eastwards over Stroud and its beech-golden valley, and across it to the line of the Nailsworth valley, hidden from almost every other viewpoint. This solitude, variety, height and spread are little known to locals and to almost all visitors. It is a trouble to get here. Very few come.

The escarpment, whose soil will grow little else, is famous for long-established beech woods, and this aerobatic journey is best made in autumn when they are all afire. We went back to Randwick and, soon after the church, forked left for Haresfield Beacon, ran into the golden misty tunnels of Standish Woods, and out into country flaming with beech on both sides, took two left turns, and stopped at a gate against the sky. This is Cripple gate, and leads to the round, bare turf top of Haresfield Beacon. The huge promontory juts forward in the escarpment, over the main line to Gloucester and the busy traffic of the Vale. Other years I have come in summer and climbed up from the base, past the old hill fort, up to this bare turf crown.

Cows graze, there is a beacon stone and map, hawthorn bushes, a wall of burning coloured woods behind, and before you the sky and the drop. Lesser hills show on each side. Far below shines the big curve of Epney in the Severn. I could see the new motorway but no sound comes from it. The distance lengthens, farther, farther, drawn on by skeins of light and haze. Smoke rises from a farm. I heard the cows ripping the short grass, thin cries of birds, a farm bell, pheasants in the woods – all held in autumn stillness. The turf seemed bare at first, until my eye dropped from the distances and saw late clover, a tiny daisy, a wiry buttercup.

When I could bring myself to move on we took the turn to Harescombe. There had been a lot of misty rain, and the burning reflection of beech leaves in the damp air held a reflection of

150

terror as if the earth was burning. Down at the bottom, in mud a-plenty, was Harescombe mill, some farms and a tiny church in a field enclosed in woods and hills. This little stretch of country towards Cud Hill, in sheltered nooks of the escarpment formation, is quiet and could well be called undistinguished – and yet it seems rather to be caught out of the countryside world one knows, and to be smiling, absorbed and living. Barns, cottages, church, gate posts, stones in the fields, are all the same colour and texture, all speak the same unknown, sweet language that one is on the point of understanding.

To keep up high we returned briefly to the A4173 to Edge and then forked right up over Huddinknoll Hill. Nearby is Hilles, the house built for himself in 1914 by Detmar Blow, architect friend of Ruskin, and lover and worker in the Cotswolds. The land is building up to the central feature of the Cotswold edge, Birdlip Hill, Leckhampton and Cleeve Hills. Quarries mark every level. The Upton St Leonards turn took us in and out of more rich beech woods, and by hedges where the holly shoots have been saved and make lines of bright beautiful young bushes. The afternoon was wearing late when we came back once more to Cud Hill, where the escarpment curves in towards Birdlip. I saw a stone viewpoint set in a rough space near the road. Although light was getting dim I went over to it, to look across to Robins Wood Hill rising up out of the Vale of Gloucester. Near by was a big stone slab set in the ground, something strange and grave. Standing by it I read 'DETMAR BLOW and WINIFRED his wife'. Nothing else. So lonesome and aerial a spot, chosen by a name I had known and yet never known – failing light, and chill, and the stone brought a shudder and I fled.

Next morning we took up our journey on the A46 and made for Prinknash, signposted Cranham. I suppose the country is so broken here that direction breaks up too and signposters choose the nearest name. In any case, this country east of the A46 is called Paradise, so you will get where you want to in the end. The *Adam and Eve* inn here on the cliff-hanging road is a great attraction.

By Cranham and Birdlip is a beautiful area right on the escarpment edge where on one side the slope is too steep for any cultivation but the beech woods and on the other there are miles of gentle, crumpled slopes threaded with footpaths, hamlets and farms twisting and perching over quarries and small bright fields. Prinknash Abbey is a Roman Catholic monastery to which the Benedictine community from Caldey Island came in 1928. It is in Prinknash Park, a big bowl half-way down the outer wooded escarpment. The original building remains, a fine Cotswold house largely sixteenth century but with earlier parts. Then there are pottery buildings and big shop, and the new modern building with crypt church under it, begun in 1939 and finished after the war. As we came down the steep approach we saw the old house at a distance on our left and the new building staring in front, not a fair comparison I agree, but on that bright autumn morning it looked like a prison, not as amiable as Northleach prison and more compressed, all the yellow stone and rows of little windows detailed in the sun. But of course this prison opens on interior worlds and is a release voluntarily sought. I walked across the big bowl of country opening onto the Vale of Gloucester, listened to the chaffinches and the quiet, and went into the crypt church.

We took the Cranham road off the A46. These woods in autumn! They made me feel those detailed, brilliant medieval paintings which I had often passed over in galleries, but which take as their secret subject all the glories shed on man and the tensions of his efforts. Cranham is up and down, mixed old and new Cotswold, perched on humps, curving on a hairpin turn in a rise. I looked from side to side dazzled with burning glory. Did the business man Joseph Horlick feel something of the terror of glory, that he has on his gravestone in Cranham churchyard 'Gone to meet the great I AM'?

Cranham Common rises behind the village. Here is held the deer feast, a medieval ceremony connected with the enlarging of the church by a wool-stapler in the fifteenth century. He left his mark in two pairs of one-handed sheep-shears on the outside of the west wall. Wool sales were conducted on the table-top tomb at the base of the tower. The feast is held over the weekend nearest to the sixth of August. After many contemporary changes of detail and costume it has settled at present for Victorian dress. There is a procession to church, an open-air all-denominational service, then the feast where the Lord of the manor and the Commoners (with rights on the Common) eat roast venison, which has been roasting whole for perhaps two days. There is a Christmas festival too, at the *Royal William Hotel*, opened by foresters in costume, and waits.

Looking from Cranham across into the vale, Cooper's Hill can be seen, where on the spring bank holiday they have a mad cheese-rolling race down the hill, a relic maybe of an old games meeting. Nearer rises High Brotheridge, an Iron Age fort of some 200 acres. The continuous woodland from Standish ends here in a spread of woods, each distinct and prized: Brockworth and Witcombe towards the vale along the escarpment, and Buckholt, Cranham and Buckle Woods on the road and edge. This forest road leads you to Birdlip, at once a prehistoric viewpoint for a crossing of the Severn, the entrance into the Cotswold hills seen and used by the Romans for their essential road joining their camps at Corinium (Cirencester) and Glevum (Gloucester), a cleft of memorable views and land formation, and an unpopulated area where much common land was established and still remains.

Birdlip Hill road plunges down to the vale from the *Royal George Hotel*, but to keep on the Cotswolds we zig-zagged past the hotel onto the A417 and came out above a big broken slope which commands a view of the spread of Gloucester city and the vale, with Cotswold outliers or single hills showing up, Robins Wood Hill, Churchdown, Chosen Hill. Crickley Hill juts forward beside Birdlip, and these two make up a long area of prehistoric settlements and forts. Barrow Wake and Shab Hill are also part of the formation. The huge bluff is all short, poor grass, dips, humps and hollows, the bushes full of small birds, the world more sky than earth, especially when you fall head-over-heels! The time I spent there on family outings, keeping out of the wind in a hollow, rolling down slopes approved to be safe, picking out streets in Gloucester or pretending to!

From Crickley the escarpment rises to Leckhampton and to Cleeve where its highest point is reached. In this central mass the little river Churn rises at Seven Springs, two miles east of Crickley Hill. The Churn is the longest tributary of the Thames, which it joins at Cricklade after passing through Cirencester. To avoid the main road to Seven Springs we turned off the A436 to a picturesque road through the first two hamlets on the Churn, Cowley and Coberley. At scattered little Cowley, the fine manor house is a county conference centre, and the superb terraced gardens are devoted to water-plant cultivation in the infant waters of the Churn. One of the most attractive country pubs is the *Green Dragon* at Cowley, where you find big log fires, a skittle alley, and the old Cotswold cordial, lovage, to drink.

At Coberley, smaller still, we went bravely through the high arched doorways of the Court on the road, into gardens and the path to the church. The great family of Berkeley from Berkeley Castle owned the manor of Coberley, and did much building here. Sir Thomas, who fought at Crecy under King Edward III in 1346, built the oldest parts of the church, and his tomb and effigy are here. So are his wife's, although she survived him, married again, and became the mother of Dick Whittington, thrice Lord Mayor of London. The only heart burial monument in the Cotswolds is here, in the sanctuary, with a small bust of a knight, also a Berkeley. He was a man of affections, for the story goes that his favourite horse, Lombard, is buried in the churchyard, where a low mound shows between path and wall. This must have been done at midnight when no bishop or abbot was looking. I was sorry to see that the mound is flatter than it used to be and looks ignored.

A short run on the A435 brought us to the main crossroad and the Seven Springs of my beloved Churn,

> clear and gentle stream
> known and loved so long.

A shallow pool lies between the stone embanked road and a green slope, beeches bending over it, holes which may be the springs, clear water moving slowly over brown-leaved bottom and pale stones. The water is piped under the road and makes a pretty pool on the other side. A curved stair of stones leads down the slope to the springs and the inscription:

> *Hic tuus O Tamesine pater septemgeminus fons*
> 'here, O father Thames, thy sevenfold spring'.

But Thames Head is in Coates parish, far from here. This claim for the Churn springs to be the source of the Thames depends on the view that the source of any river is the source of its longest tributary, which is not a claim that has to be accepted.

Now before us lay a journey we had often determined to undertake but never yet achieved – to get up onto Charlton Kings Common and see the Devil's Chimney, and then go round above Cheltenham up to the plateau of mighty Cleeve.

At the main crossroads close to Seven Springs we took the farm road on the left, behind all the AA signs. Left again where the track divides, and we set out over big open country with no roof to be seen, on an unfenced road between stubble wolds, where partridges, pheasants and small birds are the only moving thing. Nobody anywhere, so we went boldly past Hartley Farm and on into rolling miles of ploughland, until a line of larches and a little house mark a quarry where you must leave the car or bike, and follow the footpath notice to the Devil's Chimney. This tall pillar of limestone is an outstanding feature and subject of photographs and postcards. When Cheltenham was being enlarged in the late eighteenth century into the beautiful town we know, the building stone was quarried up on the Leckhampton and Charlton Kings Hills. It was brought down by horse tramroad, of which many remains can be found. Early pictures show the track going immediately behind the Devil's Chimney, and the surrounding rock quarried away, probably a fancy of the quarrymen. Erosion is at work along its vertical joints, and the chimney may fall before the end of the century. Perhaps we shall have less of the Devil's workings after that.

From here, as you fight to stand against the wind, you get a

155

famous view, not only over the vale and Cheltenham to the Malverns, but up the cliff-line of the Cotswolds, which cannot easily be seen from elsewhere. Here are the enormous quarry works, the stone from which now stands in Cheltenham's terraces and squares. Trees or bushes grow only in the quarried hollows. Over the whole plateau there is just soil enough to support tough turf. It is ideal for horseriding, but otherwise only the stone-coloured sheep with their thick coats and low, compact shapes seem natural to the harsh country.

The highest rise is still ahead, the other side of Cheltenham, on Cleeve Hill, Cloud and Common. Although it is not a matter of climbing Mount Snowdon, and although we could see Cleeve all the time in the distance, it was extraordinarily difficult to find the way there by road. We had previously tried coming off the A46 half-way up the escarpment near Southam, to find ourselves toiling up to half-grown ridges with the high land still retreating. There are no roads on the eastern approach, only wonderfully beguiling lanes and tracks. Charles worked out a way by going back to Seven Springs and taking the A436 through farm and woodland wolds of 600ft to 700ft all the way to the *Kilkenny Inn*. A nice inn-sign of sheep, a dog and a crook suits the country. Then we went through Dowdeswell, where big white ducks stroll on the verge and a long wall lines the estate of Dowdeswell Court. Down onto the main A40, right at the picturesque Cheltenham reservoir and left for Whittington, a tiny, quiet spot of great antiquity. Whittington Court is on the site of a Roman villa, and of a later fortified house of which the moat remains. The present house, with barn and stables, was built in the sixteenth century and is a beauty. We could not go into the church because a funeral was taking place, but I know it to be Norman in origin and full of local charms. Further on, in the village street, nothing has coarsened the gentle presentation of a line of sixteenth- to nineteenth-century cottages. They have mod cons, and have maintained their own beauty as well.

Soon after Whalley Farm we turned right, and kept on for two or three miles through a valley of extraordinary, out-of-this-world primitive character. Suddenly we saw the vale and

156

Cheltenham far below. Beeches have grown, blown all one way in a long line. Up at 1,000ft we looked out on a misty sea of west Gloucestershire. Cleeve Cloud stood out on the left of the narrow-banked, yellow-grassed road. Radio masts appeared. As we bumped onto rough land the road ended, all roads ended. We got out of the car, and felt it so.

Walking across the thin turf of Cleeve Common we approached the line of Cleeve Cloud on our left, with the conical shape of Cleeve Hill behind it. The Winchcombe entrant valley showed down on the right. The level land carries only archaic imprints, tiny divided sheep hooves, and round pony and horse hooves. Riders pass at a distance, birds high above sound shrill. As, chill and shivering, we approached the edge, rays came from a hidden sun through cloud on a pink sky mist. They diffused pale sunshine on a bleak land. In the far vale the big outliers of Oxenton and Dumbleton hills stood up out of dimness. On the edge we felt half dizzy – as when one stands above the English Channel on a cliff edge of the South Downs – to see the huge vale, the misty pattern of Cheltenham, the endless lines of green hedge and wooded clumps beyond. Larks twittered without noticing us. Blue breaks lightened in the heavy sky. The sheep began their long formations to gather for shelter for the night.

On these great highlands the woolly mammoth and rhinoceros once hunted for a living. Their skeletons were carried by glaciers in the last Ice Age into the present gravel-bearing valley of the Thames. Our gravel-pit workers at South Cerney dredged them up in the 1960s, and our local history group had enormous interest in collecting and studying skulls, teeth, thigh bones and joints, getting good-hearted Cirencester schoolmasters and Bristol University professors to give advice, talk to groups, and make suggestions on storage. We put on a splendid exhibition with drawings by village artists in the village hall. I thought of these great creatures as we walked along the edge of the height.

Next day Charles and I went on, from Whittington and Andoversford to Shipton Solers and Shipton Oliffe. Shipton – 'Sheepton' – and truly this has always been sheep

157

country. In the thirteenth century, Winchcombe Abbey owned a chain of manors for sheep rearing in the ten or so miles across the Cotswolds through the Shiptons to Northleach. After this, the Black Death (appeared 1348) brought a significant fall in the population, and even abandonment of some settlements in these central wolds.

Shipton, Shipton Oliffe and Shipton Solers are dotted along a stream that here joins the Clevely brook which becomes the Coln 3 miles south at Withington. Taking it as seen from the road, it makes a shallow watersplash in the farm and cottage setting of Shipton Oliffe, runs through the manor house open land and becomes a sweetness, an enjoyment of little falls and footbridge through the wilder gardens of Shipton Solers' big house. On the road opposite Shipton Solers' church is a cowshed with stone pillars and roughly cut capitals supporting the lintel beam – a Cotswold treasure I like to go out of my way to see.

The Shiptons may be small, but from their sheltering roofs our road north led into pretty well uninhabited country. The Salt Way toils across these wolds, keeping a near-straight line over the top to carry salt to the farms for animals to lick, for preserving and cleaning, for outdoor and domestic use. The road comes from the Droitwich salt area and climbs onto the Cotswolds at Hailes Abbey near Winchcombe and crosses over east to Lechlade (the Thames) and south to Cirencester. (At South Cerney, in my childhood after the 1914-18 war, the salt cart, canvas-hooded, came once a year and my mother bought twelve long blocks and kept them in the airing-cupboard.)

From Shipton we crossed the A436 to take a little road parallel to the Salt Way that passes through a few hamlets which cling like birds' nests in the rough wolds – Syreford where the old mill remains with complete machinery and wide millpond, Sevenhampton, Brockhampton. Sevenhampton has a curious church. The tower was added after the building was up, and flying buttresses cross the transepts inside to support it. Ropes and sallies show that the bells are rung here under the tower. An oddly worded inscription says that Walter Lawrence was of an ancient and respectable family which came to

158

The Market Hall at Dursley. A quiet picture of a usually busy scene. The hall has stone pillars and arches, a stone course and roughcast surface. Coat of arms on this side; Queen Anne's statue on the other faces the west end of Dursley church and tower

top The Adam and Eve under snow in Paradise near Painswick. Scotch firs and box bushes hold the snow, beeches shed it; *bottom* Spring brings the daffodils along the Leach at Eastleach clapper bridge. Eastleach Martin church has seen more than 900 Cotswold springs

England and settled here in AD 1067. In October I found the church decorated for harvest, rich and blooming. Brockhampton, a long, rambling farming spot, has a very nice inn, the *Craven Arms*, off the road in a yard behind houses, local, warm and friendly with bread and cheese for travellers. The head office of the Dowty group of engineering companies is in Brockhampton Park, and has brought with it some careful new housing.

A doubtful proposition, if not swindle, of long ago drew us off our road to the A436 over Naunton Downs to Cloud Hill and then left to Tally-Ho. Overgrown quarries hide their shame behind the hedge, and down the slope in an open space backed by woods, are some old empty cottages and bits of stone and junk. Here in 1812, for a year or two, a company made pipes out of the local limestone to provide Manchester with water from the river Medlock. Sixty miles of pipe were made, of various bores, and the company made good money out of Manchester, until people realised that the stone would not hold water and that the directors knew it. Pipe Cottages were built here for the workmen and there is a stone pipe still in the hedge wall. Not surprisingly, no Cotswolder was on the board. They may be no honester than the rest, but they would reckon everyone knew about limestone, and a low-grade quarry at that.

From Tally-Ho we followed one of the Cotswolds' beautiful dry valley roads, perfectly smooth, undulating, private, to Hawling. The sky was clearing, light spreading and making the suave surfaces look like velvet. Clean white sheep here were much bigger than those on Cleeve and Charlton Kings Commons, though black-tipped in ears, eyes, muzzle and knees. What thick coats, winter coming! Little Hawling is very pretty, a street, fine house and mighty barn. The parish absorbed the survivors of Roel whose numbers fell below subsistence in the fourteenth century. All that is left is the name, Roel Gate, just a track and road-crossing on the Salt Way, the most desolate point in all this lonely country. And yet there is fascination and power in the absence of all things human, and in the accumulation of distance on every side. Harvested fields spread red and brown among spinneys of bushes. Eight partridges landed suddenly and disappeared against the brown, stone-flecked earth. Fire lines glowed in stubble across a valley. A grey ring on the opposite side was Charlton Abbots.

We made for it, in order to reach the approach to the long barrow of Belas Knap. It is a tiny place on steep slopes, the manor house up and the church down, looking over the valley. Pheasants were shrieking in the churchyard and teetering on headstones. But the churchyard was still a burial place with green mounds, and not too mechanically spruced up. The church is simple too, a round tub of a font from the thirteenth century and a tortoise stove which looked just as homely.

From here we could see the 900ft wold into which Belas Knap is built. Of all the neolithic remains in the British Isles the Cotswold-Severn chambered tombs are among the most important, and of these Belas Knap is chief. The period 3000-2000 BC is given for these works, which makes Belas Knap about 5000 years old. The path up is marked from the road. It is long, steep and often muddy, but clearly posted. Slowly we left all comfort behind, and on the top the full force of the wind off Severn hit us. Inland, bare turf and grey field walls stretched featureless out of sight. Under the wind faint cries of swirling rooks increased the silence. Hawthorn copses clung to the steep slope and a stile brought us to the long green mound.

It is stone wall based, with horns of stone walls, and a ditch and path all round. The base wall and the horns are of dry-stone Cotswold building, no mortar, exactly as Cotswold masons have been building since these have stood here. The stones are perfectly chosen and shaped for a curving wall, thin, matched and even. You can pass your hand over the surface of stone, space, stone, and your hand would not know it was not built last year in your village. Those ancient hands were disciplined by the nature of stone, and were masters of it. Uncouth tools limited what they did, but not how they did it. Continuity like this, not only of life, but of man's work, his kinship with his material, a reciprocal, developing life through use and skill, is precious.

The horns of the tomb are not the entrance. I walked round and found it, crouched inside and heard the blood sing in my

162

ears and rejoiced that I was alive in this place of the dead. The series of chambers are made of unshaped stones half as tall as a person, and joined by enormous lintels. All the stones are of primitive enormousness, and experts speak of the architectural and engineering skill shown in the construction.

I have never been up here when there was no wind. But the distances draw the eye, even in rain squalls, away over Winchcombe to the west, further and further as faint lines come up one behind another. One can never feel one has seen to the limit. The road to Winchcombe is clear from Belas Knap footpath, and we were glad to get there after this long journeying in lonely country.

The tour described in this chapter falls within OS 1:50,000 maps Nos 162 (Gloucester and Forest of Dean) and 163 (Cheltenham and Cirencester)

Northern Wolds to Campden

Winchcombe is built like Wotton-under-Edge along a slope at the base of the escarpment and, like Wotton, is a town of oddities: Winchcombe has its own river, its own saint, was a king's capital and a centre of pilgrimage. Being aside from the main Cotswold grouping it keeps itself to itself. Backed by the heights of Belas Knap, it looks across the rich horticultural country of the vale of Evesham to the blue line of the Malverns.

Its river, the Isbourne, a working lass, springs from high up in the escarpment, one source at Postlip a mile and half away, and one in the high land behind nearby Sudeley. It runs neglected along the length of the town and then straight across the vale to join the Avon at Evesham. The saint was young Prince Kenelm of the ninth century, handed a poisoned stirrup cup by his beautiful stepsister; the kings were kings of Mercia, the central kingdom between Northumbria and Wessex from the seventh to the ninth centuries, when Winchcombe even had a mint. It became a site for pilgrimage not only to the tomb and chapel of St Kenelm but on a far bigger international scale to the abbey of Hailes outside the town. Besides all this, Winchcombe Abbey and Hailes Abbey were big landowners and employers, raising sheep, weaving and exporting woollen cloth. Sudeley Castle, close to Winchcombe, was a royal castle, and brought great men to the town. So one can understand that Winchcombe is not entirely as other Cotswold towns.

Today, Winchcombe is a simple, friendly place, two-storeyed narrow streets, corners not demolished for traffic, its church tower holding every view in unity. It has no central market place or building like most Cotswold towns, but is more like Burford, Blockley or Wotton-under-Edge. You can walk along its central street, called in turn Hailes Street, High Street, Abbey Terrace, Gloucester Street and Cheltenham Road, as a pilgrim in any century has done, and find, in the neighbouring

164

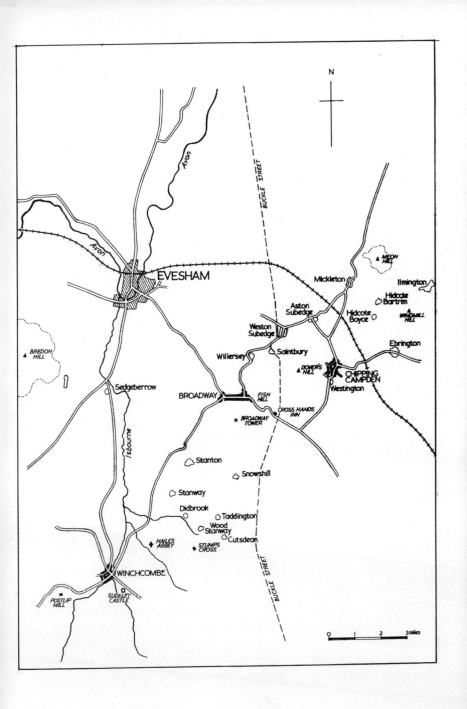

of old and new buildings, gateways, yards, alleys, hanging signs, your own interest and delight. Nearly all are built of golden stone from Cleeve Hill or local quarries, with stone-tiled roofs and little dormer windows. Many have beautiful plain porches and bow windows. In Gloucester Street you can buy Gloucestershire dripping cakes.

At the main crossroads is the galleried *George Hotel*, with the *White Hart* behind, and the Town Hall with its old stocks in the courtyard. Duck Street is lined with very picturesque cottages. Queen Square, seventeenth century, is wider and more elegant and contains the Jacobean House. Next door are the Chandos almshouses of 1573.

Both Winchcombe Abbey and Hailes Abbey have disappeared, their stones used in many buildings of the town. The parish church remains as a glory on the Abbey Terrace section of the main street. Its long roof and nave line, set with pinnacles, crenellations and caricature gargoyles, its big porch and tower, make a marvellous sight among the small houses. One of the big wool churches of the fifteenth century, it is plain and dignified like Chipping Campden's, with no sense of clutter or burden made of history. Through six nave windows and twelve clerestory windows on each side, a greenish light fills the whole quiet space right up to the splendid roof, held up effortlessly by the angels at corbel ends. There is no chancel arch, so the east end is open to the eye. Of many treasures, the chief is the altar-cloth worked from much earlier material by Queen Katherine of Aragon while living at Sudeley Castle in the 1500s.

Beside the church is a school of 1857, with a touching group of figures expressing that generation's faith in education. The Sudeley almshouses, an excellent work of Sir Gilbert Scott in 1865, run back from the school.

There is a good deal of scattered building, and many small industries and crafts thrive here. Postlip mill, noted in the Domesday Book, has been making paper since 1729, and today the company, in a thoroughly modernised mill, makes it for industrial uses. The water of the Isbourne is vital to the business because it is particularly free from iron, which can cause marking in paper. Winchcombe mill now packs flour, having ground it for 800 years.

At the other end of the town is Finch's, or the Winchcombe, pottery. There has been a country pottery in the old red brick sheds in the orchard on this corner for centuries, making slipware by hand. Slipware is earthenware on which a creamy clay is applied while the base is damp; then fired, then a glaze applied and a second firing. A lower temperature can be used than for other pottery. In most works this process became mechanized, but here it kept going in the old way all through the industrial revolution and out into modern times. Before the war the pottery was observed by Raymond Finch, who saw its value and took it on. Now it is well-known but still traditional.

I called there early on a sunny morning – mud in the lane, birds and apples in the old trees, a lantern hanging on a bough, a small red-and-white brick kiln-chimney in a corner, white wooden doors. I knocked, then opened on Raymond Finch with a mug of coffee. He showed me the ladder stair to the showroom. Wood turning is also done in one of the buildings, and the work was on show with all the delicious dark, rich-coloured potter's ware. I went down and tried another door. Two young men were stacking cream-coloured plates and bowls for firing, putting little chocks in to keep them level, in front of an open kiln made of brick with domed roof, already half-stacked. Raymond Finch's son said that the creamy ware would turn dark reddish in the firing. They make their own glaze. The fuel is wood, off-cuts from a saw-mill.

Another craft's nest is down Castle Street in the middle of Winchcombe, over the Isbourne bridge, in Tanyard Bank house on the left. On the gate are listed lettering, glass-engraving, sculpture and metal work, with the names of Bryant Fedden, famous in his own country for the first two, and Keith Jameson. The Tanyard across the road is an old industrial site beside the water. The building has an ashlared stone base and timber shuttering at the top (to let the air in and the smell out, I guess).

I leaned on the bridge and looked at the dark clear stream, Tanyard Bank's green slope down to it, kids' playthings lying about, bullfinches flashing in the snowball bushes leaning half

167

across the water, and red apples fallen in a ring round a tree on the grass.

> There had been an apple fall
> As complete as the apple had given man.
> The ground was one circle of solid red.
>
> May something go always unharvested!
> May much stay out of our stated plan,
> Apples or something forgotten and left,
> So smelling their sweetness would be no theft.

The castle mansion of Sudeley stands a short mile above Winchcombe, up a winding leafy road. The bones of its history are well known: castle rebuilt in the fifteenth century; a Tudor country estate; Princess Elizabeth spent time here; the last home of Katherine Parr, the wife of King Henry VIII who comforted his last years, married again, died here in childbirth and is buried in the chapel, now the parish church; the siege and battle for it in the Civil War, and its subsequent decay; its rescue, with Katherine Parr's rooms intact, by Emma Dent-Brocklehurst, and part restoration, part bringing to life by a selection of priceless and personally chosen items of history, art and pleasure, secured in the generation before the rage for collecting began, and including paintings, Princess Elizabeth's christening robe, and King Charles's despatch box carried round in the Civil War. Sudeley Castle is still owned by the Dent-Brocklehurst family, and in 1974 was the setting of the BBC's long serial film *The Pallisers*.

Visitors are welcomed with bird-pond, tithe barn, aviary and restaurant; the old grounds spread on a western slope with long views and huge trees. The Queen's Garden lies sunk, stone-paved, dreaming blue and silver and purple with a gentle fountain, centuries-old yew hedges cut with many openings and above them the silhouettes of Tudor arches or windows against the sky in autumn profile.

Autumn draws slowly into winter on the Cotswolds. I have always liked the winter in England, and I particularly like

168

Cotswold winter. I like the pattern of bare trees on the smooth wolds, the light-holding colour of barn, wall and house in rain or dull days, the brilliant green of turnip fields, chimney smoke among the network of brown beech branches. These are all exhilarating and eye-opening, just as the absence of many people is releasing. So I don't hesitate to write of winter journeys, even if showplaces are sometimes closed. Nowadays winter breaks are much more usual. Guest houses and cheaper accommodation have revived, hotels are generally open to the end of the year and lounges have big open fires.

Sudeley Hill road is one way up the escarpment and at the top goes over Salter's Hill to join Salter's Lane, by which the salt carts came up onto the high wolds, getting a fine view of Sudeley and of Winchcombe streets and church tower. Here are proper working farms and cottages, woods, big dips with round wolds rising out of them like pudding basins. I was last here on a pure water-colour day, brilliant and soft. I longed to seize a brush and mix myself in with it somehow. Many sheep are raised up here and the job of shepherd must be as interesting as it is necessary. I saw big flocks feeding on swedes on bare earth, with no grazing. A crow colony shone green and black among brown stubble, pheasants red-brown. A gated road opened down rich country of orchards and reddish plough, and a true picturesque farm, barns and outbuildings all stone-tiled, glowed in the winter sun.

Salter's Lane drops steeply down the escarpment in utter remoteness and silence to the site of Hailes Abbey in a wide bowl of orchards and wooded hills. Little remains of the abbey but stone markers of the foundations, a line of cloister ruins and a small museum. But the little twelfth-century church (older than the abbey) at the entrance is made of simple treasures. We saw the light stone roof, little bellcote and soft apricot stone walls against a thin blue sky. The low door invited us to step down into the stone-flagged nave. The place is archaic and gentle, with a fresh delight in delicate wall paintings of heraldic designs and feminine saints looking shyly at monks among leafy twirls, and a scene depicting men and greyhounds and a hare hiding under a bush. Small old tiles, a tiny choir, a box pew, an eight-sided orange stone font – all this has the same sense of the spirit shining through the plain holy frame as at Inglesham. The great King Edward I rode here in his old age in 1301 to the funeral of his cousin Edmund, and his coat-of-arms in the church shows it.

Down below Hailes, by the railway, we had an unusual view of the Cotswolds as a bold green wall to the north along the vale. Then we climbed back into Stanton and Stanway country. Wold and vale meet in Didbrook, the first village. Houses are built of stone, plastered brick and dark timber. One even shows the very old cruck construction, with two big tree-trunks curved into a wish-bone shape at each end. Orchard, cows and mud all looked like a painting in winter sunshine. Wood Stanway is in apricot stone, its high-banked hedges with ferns still green, the stream channelled by the road with stone steps over. Sturdy barn, spreading farm buildings, stone cottages, working people about, buff hens and stacks of bean-pole timber under orchard trees, elms still clear-yellow leaved, tall against the green and brown spread of the vale; there is no better sight.

Stanton, outstandingly beautiful, was fortunate in its modern squire, Sir Philip Stott the architect. He saw its untouched and vulnerable beauty and settled here in 1906. For thirty years he eased Stanton into modern times. After Stott's death the local council built some houses in traditional style, stone walls and stone-tiled roofs. Stanton was then secured as a Cotswold jewel, a joy for all to see and potter round. Not being on a main road, it is saved from poor Broadway's ossifying.

I saw Stanton Court gardens on one of their open days, enchantingly laid out for prospects and nooked for courting, brooks led in step-falls through water-garden and pool and ornamental canal. Here was a tree-lupin, alone on a long lawn, a tall perfect cone of yellow and green. Every straggling bushy one I have grown since has been to me a far contact with that Stanton perfection.

The Court is not a 'great house' like Stanway, but a richly designed and quiet early seventeenth-century country mansion, its garden wall right on the village street. The church is

170

another little Cotswold delight, a seven hundred years' blend of high life and country life, dim with dark wood and stained glass (modern by Comper) and crisply carved Norman pillars. There is a very rare survival of a timber pulpit of the fourteenth century, and also one of 1684 from which Wesley preached. The back pew-ends show marks of the ropes of shepherds' dogs. They must have heard the word of the lost sheep and the ninety-nine left in the wilderness – in care of a dog, of course.

From the old cross up, the village street is all built in golden-buff stone and dark tiles, with semi-circular steps rising up to many cottages. The little school stands among the houses. Everywhere one sees the cherished details of drip-moulds over windows, stone mullions, tiles, dormer windows, and here and there dates cut on door lintels, '1604 JOHN JAMES', 1615, 1618. Between cottages one catches glimpses of sheep on high grass banks, even in a scattering of snow.

The street becomes a track and climbs up to the *Mount* inn, passing a signpost to the Cotswold Way, a long-distance es-carpment public footpath. The inn has a most spectacular site, perched high above the village. On our December day the stone-flagged bar had a log fire and hot, home-made, in-dividual loaves for ploughman's lunch. In summer time we have sat outside on this ledge of the land and seen rising out of the vale of Evesham, the great humps of Dumbleton Hill and Alderton Hill, Cotswold outliers, and beyond, the long back of Bredon Hill, landscape old in poetry, song and story. You'll hear some English stories today in the *Mount*'s public bar.

'Pigeons! ... 'e 'ad 200 pigeons just for research, flyin' research, he put contact lenses in its eye, 'e 'ad a battery on one and a magnet an' when 'e released it, it flew right in the opposite direction, an' when the battery ran down it turned round and flew 'ome'.

Last time I was here a country workman said earnestly to me, speaking of Stanton Court and the landowner, 'When you get a family like that as takes a real interest in the *land*, that's worth something. Nothing left to chance, they do it as it should be

171

did.' That was certainly the way the little houses of Stanton were built.

In early summer the road to Stanway and the hill country round Stanton are a bright world of laburnum. It seems to have naturalised itself here into a field tree, as I have seen nowhere else. Stanway is mainly the magnificent house and the tithe barn, a few cottages and a village hall designed by Detmar Blow. The tithe barn is one of the most impressive of all barns, its incredible stone roof supported by cruck frames bedded into the walls with massive braces. It has two porches, and gables with stone finials. Standing in fine parkland where the scale of tree and space is big, its size only creeps on one slowly. It was built in the fourteenth century for another abbot, of Tewkesbury this time. Occasionally it is used for dramatic or musical performances.

The road leaped from Stanway up through a tree world, winter vistas streaming past us through the trunks as we got nearer and nearer the sky. Suddenly trees fell away and we were on Stumps Cross, another vacant, unhoused crossroads on Cotswold heights. At near 800ft, a cliff of apricot stone stared at us, with crust of turf and hawthorn, layers of huge stones, piles of crushed stone, gravel and sand – Guiting Quarry, in production. We saw it in a calm hour of December twilight, when one almost sees winter itself, to catch without seeking it

> her sigh
> and solemn, gathering tear,
> and look of exile from some deep repose, the sphere
> of ether, moved by ether only, or
> by something still more tranquil.

The glow from the golden quarry-face spread into the fading air, and over a wold side covered by sheep which glimmered in it. Down another slope I could see Cutsdean, just becoming invisible as the lines and colours of its roofs returned to the soil contours from which they were raised.

Next morning we went north from here on the road through Taddington, with Stanway Ash plantation marking the long

172

escarpment crest at 900ft, through fields of bright green winter sprouts and miles of dark soil winter-sown. Tumuli mark the slopes. Shenberrow fort lay almost 1,000ft up on our left, above Stanton. There was not a house to be seen, and the wolds were still rising, when we climbed through a patch of broken country and dropped down into Snowshill. The main street climbs up again to a street line along the crest and another just below, which gives the place a look of having spilled over the top. The village is all stone and very old, though ugly housing-estate windows have spoiled a house in a telling point on the main street. Being so high and lonely, the place is full of air and silence, with rooks cawing in a rookery in tall trees which now in winter made a transparent pattern on the sky. Houses built on random humps look as if they had grown out of them overnight. The *Snowshill Arms* is a Donnington pub, so worth remembering. The big house here is Snowshill Manor, a National Trust property of about 1500, long used as a farmhouse. It keeps an old countrified feel inside, and houses collections of toys, bicycles, musical instruments. The small gardens are terraced on the steep drop, and contain a dovecote.

From Snowshill we went north through high, open, uncompromising country. A great many horses were being reared on big slopes near a farm, and I wondered whether they would winter out-of-doors. December was not really cold, but what would January and February be like up here? Yet the Cotswolds are not, as de Quincey said of the Lake District, 'too oppressive, in their colossal proportions and their utter solitudes, for encouraging a perfectly human interest'. We turned into Buckle Street, a native pre-Roman (perhaps pre-wheel, only for man and pony) road over the wolds at high level. Here sheltered by Broadway Wood, it leads past a local viewpoint and curiosity, Broadway Tower, which stands above Broadway at 1,031ft, second highest point in the Cotswolds. It was built in 1798 by the Earl of Coventry. All follies are interesting, and in this one William Morris, D. G. Rossetti and Edward Burne-Jones spent a holiday. It consists of a graceful central tower with three small round outer towers, windows and balconies in the centre, all in a light grey stone. On one of our bright, thin-air winter days

173

one can see fifty miles each way, to the Wrekin in Salop, Border Hill in Leicestershire, White Horse Hill in Oxfordshire, the Brecon Beacons in Powys.

This rough hill and surrounds is now being made into a picnic area, so there is the more reason to see it first in winter. The levels have been too rough and the soil too poor for cultivation all through the centuries, so that the plough has not destroyed old formations, levelled the characteristics or caused boundaries to be altered. Some of the dry stone walls date from the fifteenth century. Certainly the cold, the humps of grey stone, the rough hollows, the short yellow-green turf marked by myriad tiny split hooves, the tangled hawthorn bushes, must be exactly as they were five hundred years ago. You may shiver into your coat, but the white-faced sheep gaze placidly at you and go on munching, one behind the other in long lines into the wind.

Buckle Street crosses the Oxford road that leads down into Broadway. The picnic area spreads to here. You can see from the main road a stone viewpoint and a track marked to it. This carries a relief map in slate of the whole view, the rivers and hills beautifully cut and named. The inscription says it is placed here in memory of Alderman Russell and his constant care for the amenities of the county.

From this point, going slowly down Fish Hill (the main road) there is the most spectacular view of Broadway – the roofs below, the blue-green vale of Evesham beyond, and Bredon's long shape of lovers, bells and poetry, the Malverns behind, and faint and clear still more hills. Broadway is a famous beauty spot, but being only a small place on the main Stratford-Oxford road, it seems to me to have been unable to keep personality. I used to love it, and of course there it still is, beautiful houses, beautiful stone, faultless flowers all the summer, a wonderful setting of wolds and vale – yet too much white paint, and a crushing pressure of traffic and strangers all hungry for the same round of shops, cafés, hotel lounges, glimpses. However, there are always the Gordon Russell workshops where chairs and furniture are made in simple good design, of wood with much hand work and beautiful finish. All

174

Northleach's church chairs were made here. In winter too, there is room for the schoolchildren and mothers and prams, the holly trees are afire with berries, the Globe Players from Stratford may be doing a miracle play or the choir will be giving a carol service, and winter musical weekends are held in the splendid old hotel the *Lygon Arms*.

Out on the Stratford road, little Willersey holds its Cotswold character, in spite of the flat vale and the traffic. The *Bell* inn and the village pond with white ducks are a joy. But this is the Cotswold limit on the vale road, and we sprang with joyful release back up the escarpment again by Fish Hill to the Chipping Campden turn, called Cross Hands. Set back on the verge against the young woods that line the road is a queer 7ft tall fingerpost, dated under two of the fingers 1669. This was put up by Nathan Izod of Westington, Chipping Campden. The arms are forged in iron and end in fingers. Cut on them is THE WAY TO OXFORD XXIII MILES 1669, and THE WAY TO WOSTER XVIII MILES N. I., and so on. N.I. stands for Nathan Izod. The distances are a little out. Roman numerals were still more commonly used and read in 1669 than the modern arabic, except, I take it, for dates. Chedworth was clearly well ahead. The fingerpost is one of the very few of its date still left.

Charles Williams used to say that if one gave thanks before bodily food, one could give it before reading Milton, and I would give it also before the hill sight of Chipping Campden. A mile or so from Cross Hands, as we came out from the screen of woods on the left, we caught the afternoon light on the high wolds and the field walls. In the dip below shone the tower of Chipping Campden church, and all the buff walls and olive-brown roofs of the houses. Ahead, Meon Hill's crest reminded us of our journey's end. There was not a pylon in sight. Every morning, and in late afternoon, the stone top of wall, chimney or roof is caught in the sun. That day, dense green fields of sprouts lined the road in strong colour. We drove slowly down the hill into Westington, once separate from Campden, with its own manor fields and house, then wound into Campden's Sheep Street and High Street. We stayed three nights here in December shortly before Christmas, at the *King's*

Arms which we had known before.

It was dark by the time we had settled in and had tea by an open fire. We set out then to look at Chipping Campden. Non-distorting street lights showed up the green verges, low gables and arched doorways; stone-flagged yards had their lights on; all along High Street small shop windows were scarlet-bright and tinselly with Christmas goods and decorations, individual, fresh and enticing. Next morning it was just as good. Campden was busy with school coaches and shopping. I smelt bread baking, and found the baker. A few doors away was the up-to-date window display of Robert Welch's Old Hall table-ware, the designs for which he produces in Campden. He also has a showroom for designers and artists of distinction. I saw Silk Mill on Cam stream in Sheep Street, where Hart's silver and metal business is carried on, one of the original crafts set up in Silk Mill in 1902.

High Street curved invitingly ahead. The Market Hall of 1627 stands on pillars, short and strong in mid-street, throwing black shadows and bright street glimpses through its arches, as at Tetbury, Minchinhampton and Dursley. The whole street is a harmony of golden-buff stone, in gables, tall chimneys, archways, pediments and pillars, mullioned or sash windows, big flat stone steps, dark olive-brown roofs high or shallow, and hanging shop signs, all on a comfortable small scale. The fourteenth-century Woolstaplers' Hall, Grevel House and the Grammar School of 1487 need attention to find because all the domestic and commercial buildings harmonise in their individual joys. The shops too are individual and high quality, some of them showing development of a specialist skill as in woollen cloth, wood or needlework. Hanging iron shop-signs add a line of detailed ornament to the street.

When the moon was up, I went out to revisit Campden's special corner. In the lower end of Church Street the three bow windows of the *Eight Bells* were curtained and warm-lighted from within as I knew it well, having first been led there by Massingham's enthusiasm. The gable top above each window was touched with pale light. Round the corner, moonlight flowed into the wide space. It lit each gable and chimney of the

176

twelve almshouses, picked out each curve of the carving on the gateway of Old Campden House and on the stately tower of the church, gleaming white through the openwork parapet. Against the wide, grey-green background of the Conygre slope, every bush and hummock threw a black shadow.

These almshouses, and Old Campden House, were built by Sir Baptist Hicks in the early years of the seventeenth century. The house was burned down in the Civil War and only the gateway and two pavilions remain. The almshouses are a wonderful piece of work, spaciously set on a rising pavement, modernised in 1959. Verey thinks them 'the crowning achievement of the domestic Cotswold style and mason craft of the early seventeenth century'. The church is a hundred years older as we see it, and parts are three hundred years older still. The stone was all brought from a quarry on Westington hill. The avenue of limes was planted in 1770, older by 22 years than Painswick's yews.

This is one of the fifteenth-century wool churches, not lavish in detail like Cirencester and Fairford, but cool and still like Northleach and Winchcombe. Indeed, it is thought that the same hands must have worked here as at Northleach. Campden history, and wider history than Campden's, is written on the brasses and local memorials of this church. The tower is striking, pure and stately in line, with Cotswold diagonal buttresses, and twelve pinnacles. Although it is built in three stages, the lines of decoration are carried boldly up through all, keeping concentration of shape. The perfect harmony of line and decoration throughout the church can elude a surface glance and be taken for coldness. I used to think it so, but the eye learns to see deeper. Line and stillness, colour and clarity, join with fifteenth-century altar hangings and carvings in the south chapel and on the pulpit, to open and inform the spirit. Cotswold craftsmen built this and added to it, and modern ones have decorated it, Norman Jewson with woodwork, George Hart with silver. The south door inside the porch has just been replaced, matching the outer door. Like its predecessors, the new door was built locally of English oak with iron studs, latch and bolt made by the smith at Kingham. A workman told us about it and about the remains of Campden House.

'You've lived in Campden all your life?' I asked.

'Ay, I was born in Campden, thank God,' he answered.

Past the church the lane curves round to the left and becomes Back Ends, parallel to High Street and joining it again below Sheep Street. Seven thatched Twine Cottages recall a rope and sack works here. All the houses or plots on this lane seem to run down to connect with the backdoors of High Street in a handy way for the shops. Above this side of Chipping Campden rises the green height of Dover's Hill.

How did this beauty come to be here, and to survive? Campden was a wool market through the Middle Ages, very prosperous and well known throughout western Europe. Its leading merchants, notably William Grevel (the brass in the church speaks of him), spent their fortunes in the town, building the church, grammar school, guild halls, inns and houses. In the seventeenth century Sir Baptist Hicks bought the manor and settled in Campden, a merchant banker, one of the founders of the Virginia Company, friend of King James I. He used his brains and his money in Campden, built the Market Hall and the almshouses, rebuilt the school, built himself Old Campden House, enriched the church with the pulpit and the brass falcon lectern. His tomb and his wife's are in black marble under a canopy in the south chapel, and the carved hands of his granddaughter in a wall tablet. He also built Campden House in Kensington, London, in 1612. At the same time, Captain Robert Dover started the games named after him on the high land outside Campden, now named properly Dover's Hill. They were designed to be an English version of the Olympic festivities of old Greece, and became vastly popular.

The wool trade declined, moved south in search of water for powered mills. Slowly Chipping Campden slipped back into village ways. Only the buildings of a busy, renaissance small town with continental trading connections remained, dreaming round the farm-working people. In 1893 Algernon Gissing saw the High Street. 'Here was the old world itself, touched by a magic wand centuries ago and still remaining spellbound. . . . Between the church tower and the sun lay the antique town in one graceful curve of what seemed infinite detail and variety yet of matchless harmony.'

Under the influence of Ruskin and Morris, thoughts on man and living were taking shape in action. In 1902 C. R. Ashbee brought a London guild of handicraftsmen to Campden, 150 people in all, and settled them in Silk Mill, Sheep Street, and cottages nearby. This began Campden's new development as a craft centre. There were classes, lectures, activities; the movement thrived and its public grew. One result was an amenity crisis, in 1926, before environmental consciousness was fully developed. Dover's Hill was put up for sale as a suitable site for a hotel. Everyone was appalled, nobody moved. Time was short. One artist, F. L. Griggs, a man with little money, sold all that he had and gave it to the poor, the poor-spirited people of Campden, moneyed and unmoneyed; he bought the land and gained time to settle it in public ownership. Now Dover's Hill, looking down into Campden, belongs to the National Trust local committee and is safe. Much of his money was collected and returned to Griggs. The time and the opportunity could not have been returned. The other green hill site, the Conygre, was similarly saved in 1934.

Since then Campden has grown gently and beautifully, and imparted life to all movements for individual craft skills throughout the Cotswolds and a wider world. It has shown that the old standards, old beauties and joys can live well in modern times, and modern times can be happier for them. Craft work extends to cooking, and good old-English fare can be found in restaurants. The town keeps its round-the-year rooted pleasures, craft-classes, bell-ringing, Morris dancing, the Christmas mumming play, the Campden Players, and the big early summer festival over the spring bank holiday. Then, on Dover's Hill Dover's Games are held again, and Scuttlebrook Wake fills the streets where the May Queen is crowned, the Morris Men dance, and for a day, the passing of centuries is no more than the turn of a page.

Dover's Hill is a view and a recreation place all the year. Between Meon Hill on the right and Bredon away on the left you can see Shakespeare's Stratford under moving cloud shadows. Up here the wind even in summer makes a delicate wing and feather sky. One can ride and walk for miles.

Come off the hill, down the lane and away to Saintbury. Half a mile along the road is the Kiftsgate Stone, one worthy to be respected because it signals the majority stirring themselves against the toughs. It was a stone of meeting by the time it was recorded. In the seventh or eighth centuries, times of violence and raiding, subdivisions of the shire which had their own courts were called hundreds, and the stone gave its name to this one, Kiftsgate Hundred. Here decisions were taken by the men of the hundred, bands met to combine against raiders, local justice was done, and here the Great Charter (Magna Carta) was read aloud to them a month after it was signed by King John in 1215. It was a point in the beginning of self-government. Such points existed in many places, but the Kiftsgate Stone survives. It stands on the edge of a wood that runs towards Buckle Street.

Turn right into Buckle Street and keep straight on. Here the old Street comes off the Cotswolds, and on its way passes through Saintbury half way down. New stables and a barn in bright beautiful timber mark the beginning of the village, and then the road bends towards the little church at the top of the street. Saintbury is nearly all seventeenth century, built of a grey stone, pure north Cotswold. There is hardly any level ground except for one cottage at a time, with a shed and a few fruit trees close by.

The church began life in early Norman days, and has a tower and slender spire which is a landmark in the escarpment. What a site for a church! The Midland plain stretches out, sunset spreads over a distance like the sea. Inside, the church is full of lovely details. A wrought-iron chandelier carries the name of C. R. Ashbee, 1911. I thought of being a Saintbury church-woman, and coming to my Christmas midnight celebration up here, and going out after it into the frost perhaps, to see the close stars and feel the infinite dark air spread light-twinkled through those distances above and below me.

Buckle Street goes down through the village, between the houses and hedges that have stood here so long. Saintbury stone tiles are of very small scale, big or little, and this gives the cottage roofs a delicate, light look. The unending differences of character and grace given by our natural stone-tile roofs to ordinary, similar cottages never struck me more clearly. The Saintbury Pedigree Herd of Ayrshires looked very beneficent, their dark brown coats splashed with white. At the bottom of the hill is the medieval cross (with modern head). The first change of sunset picked out Saintbury spire, and as we moved on, cut out Willersey tower against the west.

Weston Subedge and Aston Subedge are the last two villages on the stone base of the northern escarpment. Buckle Street strode away across the vale as we turned right onto the A46 or Stratford road for Weston. Ryknild Street also comes off the Cotswolds here as a muddy track just before Weston. Our road ran on it for a few hundred yards, and left it again. Ryknild Street then runs straight to Bidford-on-Avon.

Weston and Aston Subedge, off the main road, are very out-of-the-way villages, with good seventeenth-century houses on their small streets and farm-houses standing back. It is well worth walking round the square on which Weston mainly stands, for the shapes of hedge cutting, as well as for the charming houses. The *Seagrave Arms* gave us a proper winter's day welcome with an open fire and a lunch that a real plough-man would have approved. Aston has half-timber and brick mixed in with its stone, and a very fine seventeenth-century Manor Farm. Prince Rupert, dashing nephew of Charles I, used to stay in the manor house here for Dover's Games. Though this was December, a row of red-hot-pokers stood up against a stone wall, and roses were still out in many gardens.

Here the Cotswold formation narrows to its end. We wanted to go over the top and down on the eastern side to feel this, and come back for the last height. So, from Aston, we took the road back into Campden, then turned left for Ebrington. This is fruit-growing country, including a hillside of currants, gooseberries and soft fruit bushes. Sheep and goats always look picturesque under orchard trees, and I fancy this area is the original of many calendars and enamelled trays. Certainly I treasure an old tray picturing Ebrington, given me by a countrywoman whose mother came (reluctantly) from there.

No one seems to be willing to leave Ebrington, like the people of Ashton Keynes.

The road sinks as you come in, so that the cottages are up on banks of fern and foxglove, or on worn steps or in bowers in hollows, all mixed in with hedges and rose bushes and little paths with box bushes, one cottage in another one's garden, with steps leading from here to there without too much definition. All is gentle, easy going, easy come, sunny in winter, bosky in summer. Seats round three oaks on the little green are made for chat, and the *Ebrington Arms* beside the green completes the social centre. I was grieved to see that the village shop had closed since I was last here, though Woodbine Cottage is licensed to sell tobacco; so if any reader wants an opportunity just like this, in just this kind of place, make haste, for I am sure there is no other place like Ebrington.

It is the village of simple stories, and Cotswold humour is simple. Ebrington folk, they say, grew their hedges tall to keep the cuckoo in, and manured the church to make the tower grow. They certainly have the most peculiar clockworks under the tower, perhaps awaiting reinstatement or to strike the Last Hour. I have read that it was made by the local smith and needs winding every day, which an Ebrington villager is happy to do. A Lord Chief Justice of England settled here and has his effigy in the little Norman church, propped up by a few bricks – Sir John Fortescue of the fifteenth century. A unique memorial in the church records in 1846 a man's 'devoted attachment to three Maiden Aunts, under whose fostering care' he spent 'his earliest and happiest years'. Another is put up by six children who showed 'their abiding love of their old home at Ebrington'. The east window is modern, concerned with many races raising or making or selling bread, with Christ in the middle as the bread of life.

Across to the eastern drop is a rough solitary journey through strawberry fields and stony plough. At Charingworth we turned left up Goose Hill. More strawberries, and gates on the lane for Windmill Hill as we cross the Warwickshire boundary. The Stour valley lies below. This east-facing slope of the Cotswolds is old farm country, and big spreads of sprouts and cabbage looked fresh in December. Tractors were out pulling rollers on the slopes with piles of bags, probably fertiliser. From Windmill Hill we looked over the whole Oxford plain, fertile, green, criss-crossed with brown hedges and pointed by red farm or village roofs. Compton Wynyates lies seven miles away. The bluff edge here at 600ft is half yellow stone, half rough yellow grass, dotted with gorse bushes and tough sheep. Foxcote farm barn shows a carved arch entrance.

We dropped steeply down into Ilmington, and saw a coloured tile of a bear and ragged staff set in a house, so we knew we were in Warwickshire. (Remember the Four Shire Stone only a few miles south by Moreton-in-Marsh?). Off the high ground, everything looks a little richer, a little more varied, easy and complicated. The village straggles in a circle, mixed brick and stone, gardens noticeably pretty. A hurdle-maker carries on his business here, and on the grass verge outside the cottage he has his timber on one side and piles of white hurdles on the other. Men passed us exercising big horses. What a place of hedges, and the holly loaded with berries in gardens and churchyard! A large missel thrush and many blackbirds with a lot of white on them were busy under the trees. Here in the church I saw bright new sallies and bellropes, a notice of membership of the Four Shire Guild of Ringers, records, photographs and certificates.

The road back to Hidcote and its famous garden is halfway down the escarpment, and I could see the soil richer on the vale side and poorer on the wold side. Meon Hill stood straight ahead. A long silhouette of wind-bent trees, small beeches and firs marked the top of a rise, and when we reached it and saw no rich plains but wolds all round, we felt the relief of definition and limitation.

Kiftsgate Court is on the way. This has another memorable garden which is open on certain announced days. It specialises in roses of every kind and variety, and as if this were not enough, it has transformed a long wold side into spreading gardens, with water dropping and running through all. The edge of this garden hill can be seen from the road; it is memorable in rhododendron time.

Hidcote Bartrim, with its gardens that were a lifetime's offering and now belong to the National Trust, is clearly posted. This is a glory of the north Cotswolds, as the greater Westonbirt arboretum is of the south. We were bold to go in winter, but after some visits in other seasons we found it a good choice. Hidcote is a series of gardens. To be alone there, to have no bored children in the stone-flagged topiary under the cedar, or foot-weary parents among the Old Roses in the kitchen garden, no crowds in the quincunx of pleached hornbeams and the little pavilions, or blocking the coloured hedges used as tapestries, to have silence by the pool and fountains and in the whispering stream garden – this was wonderful. So many late autumn bushes and winter bulbs were out that I could have spent as many hours here as in the summer richness.

To approach the sentinel height of Meon Hill, we dropped down to Mickleton below Kiftsgate. We went through Hidcote Boyce to the B4081, crossing Campden tunnel on the railway, where we saw again Chipping Campden church tower and pinnacles, then turned right for Mickleton. Men were getting in late black straw-bales, and lifting potatoes. Mickleton is another border Cotswold place, looking out rather than up, brick and timber from Worcestershire coming in with the stone. The number of small, neat hotels suggests a good spot for ordinary travellers, and the soft colour of the brick gives the place a warm charm. Attractive half-timbered council houses are an asset. Medford House, in the middle of Mickleton, explains at a look what the writers mean by 'traditional gabled Cotswold', 'Queen Anne' or 'classical', and 'flat roof with dormers', because it was built in 1694 when transition of style had reached the remote countryside; Medford House has the lot.

And now, seriously as at all endings, we set out on our last journey, through Upper Clopton to Meon Hill, first and last jut of the Cotswolds above the vale of Avon and Shakespeare's Stratford. Wind-pumps and greenhouses marked the road, but as we climbed, white-faced sheep took over. The air was dense with starling formations, wheeling in hundreds as one. Bright-flecked clouds layered the sky. We left the car at a farm gate below the green back of Meon Hill, and walked up a track through fields to the climb. Wind-bent beeches, ash and hawthorn cling just below the top. Sheep with clean white long wool, long tails and speckled faces were scattered all over the hillside, moving away nibbling as we scrambled up through ledges and layers of the prehistoric settlement and fort. An occasional baa, the wind, and the pounding of blood in our ears were the only sounds. On the last ledge five sheep waited, and watched, seeming to challenge us. As we came up under their light eyes and black specked noses, they broke and cantered away to join the others.

We climbed over the fence against the sky, and were up. A scurry of belligerent blue tits whizzed past us out of the low trees. The hill crest was ploughed, light brown and stony, and swept down to the west in a perfect curve. One big tree spread in the centre, with sacks thrown under it, and on the curve against the western sky was one Scotch fir. We tramped round the yellow-brown verge of the ploughland to look out over the Midland sea. It did not look real. There was no other world than sky and hilltop, and ourselves. The wind sang in our ears and hair. The furrowed ground was closely marked with tiny hoof-prints. Far below on the hillside we saw more and yet more lines of sheep. A flutter made me look round. There was nothing to be seen but brown ploughland rising to the crest. But the flutter went on. Then I saw in the plough furrows a dry beech leaf blown violently to and fro and caught by the ridges, a tiny compelling voice of wind and earth and tree.

There is no further to go, so this is the end. Perhaps you will go home to tea and buttered toast in Stratford, or by a log fire in Chipping Campden. Wherever you go, we wish you well. You have come with us to see again these thirty miles of Cotswold hills, small towns and churches, villages and farms, clear and gentle streams, woods, sheep and plovers. We hope you will be moved to follow up the book by coming to see, then coming again and again.

The tour described in this chapter falls within OS 1:50,000 maps Nos 163 (Cheltenham and Cirencester), 150 (Worcester and the Malverns) and 151 (Stratford-upon-Avon)

Acknowledgements

I gratefully acknowledge the illustrations to the following: to W. R. Bawden, Eagle Photos, Cheltenham, plates on pages 33, 51, 70, 105(b), 106(a), 142, 159 and 160; to P. D. Turner, Frampton Mansell, Stroud, 34, 69, 87(a), 88, 105(a), 106(b), 123, 124 and 141; to David Iddles, Wotton-under-Edge, 87(b), and to the *Wilts and Gloucestershire Standard*, 52.

I also gratefully remember people through my life in South Cerney (my grandmother included) and throughout the Cotswolds, but, having to choose I want to thank my husband, Charles, who has aided me, and planned and map-read every trip and contributed his own knowledge all the way; David and Rosemary Verey, to whom all writers and plant-lovers of the Cotswolds must owe a debt; Lionel Walrond, expert in the Cotswold woollen industry and mills, and willing helper of seekers; Sonia Rolt who showed me new interests in the north Cotswolds; Richard Bradley who gave time to take Charles and me round his South Cerney and Ashton Keynes works; L. C. Arkell who did the same at his Donnington Brewery; Kenneth Buck who let me see over Bliss' tweed mill at Chipping Norton; Alan and Joan Tucker, booksellers, of Stroud, who helped me with much local knowledge of their area; and finally and indispensably, Eric Poole of Cirencester, who drove us on our expeditions, on roads good and bad, known and unknown, with equal good humour and reliability.

I also want to thank Dawn Bijl and Melanie Patton who patiently typed the manuscript.

Alice Mary Hadfield

Index

188